D0899464

Introduction to Biology

A Study by

JOHN HOLZMANN

Copyright @ 1993, 1994, 1998, 2003, 2005 by John Holzmann

All Rights Reserved

No part of this publication may be reproduced, stored in a retrieval system, or transmitted in any form or by any means—electronic, mechanical, photocopy, recording, or any other—except for brief quotations embodied in critical articles or printed reviews, without prior written permission of the publisher.

Plant illustrations on pp. 55-68 are adapted from *Plant Classification* by Lyman Benson, copyright 1957 by D. C. Heath & Co., and are used by permission. Detailed animal kingdom illustrations on pp. 74 through 119, and pp. 124 through 167 are adapted from *The Animal Kingdom*, edited by Frederick Drimmer, copyright 1954 by Greystone Press. Permission to use these latter illustrations has been sought, but current copyright owners are unknown.

Cover illustration by Drew Thurston, copyright 1998 by Sonlight Curriculum, Ltd.

Published by

Sonlight Curriculum, Ltd.
8042 South Grant Way
Littleton, CO 80122-2705
(303) 730-6292
Fax (303) 795-8668
E-mail: main@sonlight.com

Fifth Edition, May 2005

Printed in the United States of America

Table of Contents

Part 2: Classification

The Animal Kingdom (*continued*)

NOTES TO PARENTS

What this Book Is About

Science involves making observations, organizing information, forming hypotheses, and then testing those hypotheses through experiments and further observation. So I thought that since biology is a science, an introduction to biology text should tell children about some of the basic observations biologists have made down through the years. We begin with a brief look at the historical development of modern biological science, and then quickly move into a relatively detailed catalog of the major kinds of plants and animal biologists have discovered. I pray that this book will give your children a basic foundation of biology, and excite you both to want to discover more.

About Sexual Reproduction As Covered in this Book

While writing this book, it occurred to me that the first time I ever heard of sexual reproduction was when I was taught about human sexuality—during my first "sex ed" class in fifth grade.

Why was that? Plants reproduce sexually. Most animals reproduce sexually. Why did my parents (and, in my case, the public school) wait to teach me the facts about sexual reproduction until it was time to talk about the much more difficult subject of how men and women, boys and girls should treat each other?

Now here I am a parent. I have just finished a study about plants and animals. I didn't realize plants had sperms! I had never heard that term used before in the context of plants. Hmmm. So I thought: why shouldn't we talk about the wonders of sperms and eggs, fertilization, and all the other marvels of sexual reproduction *before* we have to deal with the moral issues of human relations? Why not learn the basic words and general meanings while talking about the much less emotionally-charged issues of how plants and animals reproduce? Then, by the time we get to human reproduction (in Sonlight Curriculum we cover that subject in Human Anatomy and Physiology), we can spend less time on the mechanics and more time on the issues that make a difference: how will you honor the Lord in the way you treat members of the opposite sex?

You will find in this book that I cover the basics of sexual reproduction. I use the words "sperm," "ovum," and "fertilization." When talking about animals, I talk about the difference between egg-laying and placental (within the body) growth.

I don't dwell on these topics, but I could hardly avoid them. Reproductive differences separate two whole orders of mammals from all the others.

I mention these matters now so you will be prepared when, appear in the text of this book, you come across the words that describe sexual reproduction. I believe you should be able to use them with your children without embarrassment. God has designed plants and animals in amazing ways.

A Regret

One of my sorest regrets about this book is the fact that my intended audience—elementary-age children—lacks knowledge of chemistry and genetics, and I am incapable, in the space available, to explain these subjects adequately. I regret this because biochemists, geneticists and molecular biologists keep piling up data about plant and animal chromosomes. And the more information they pile up, the more ridiculous it appears that any plant or animal could have possibly evolved from another through chance mutations and so-called "natural selection."

If you, as parent/teacher would care to do some studies in this area, I particularly recommend Davis and Kenyon's high school text, *Of Pandas and People* (Richardson, TX: Foundation for Thought and Ethics, 1989; Sonlight item #RS26) and Ian T.

Taylor's *In the Minds of Men: Darwin and the New World Order* (Toronto, Canada: TFE Publishing, 1991).

About Reading and Using this Book with Elementary Age Children

There are a lot of scientific words in this book—many more than you will find in the average elementary school biology text. And I can imagine you may want to curse me for the fact that I use them.

I pray you don't. I pray, instead, that you will consider them a blessing.

A large portion of true science education consists of learning new words. It must consist of such learning. Why? Because words and concepts go together.

"Cotyledon," for instance, is a scientific word; it is also a concept. You can hardly master the concept if you don't have a word for it.

Without appropriate vocabulary, you end up merely pointing to things and saying, "See that thing there?"

"Yes. And what did you want to tell me about 'that thing there'?"

"Well, it's like that other thing over there!"

Obviously, conversation like this won't get you very far. Why not call both "things" what they are: "cotyledons," "stamens," "pistils," or whatever?

"But," you may say, "my children can't handle all these new words. In fact, I'm not sure I can remember all the words!"

Please don't worry. Your children don't have to "pass a test" ten weeks from today. Indeed, they don't even have to pass a test this evening. I wouldn't expect my children to remember all this vocabulary—tonight or tomorrow, much less at the end of the school year.

However, at the end of the day, when your spouse comes home, perhaps your children can show off some of their newfound knowledge. "Look, Dad (or Mom)! See this? This is a seed. It has several parts to it. See this thing here? It's a . . . – Oh!

I can't remember its name. What is it, Mommy (or, Daddy)? . . ." —And maybe you'll provide the answer. Or maybe you won't. (Maybe you won't because maybe *you* won't remember the word! [It's *cotyledon*.]) But whether you do or you don't, your child will continue with his or her narrative. . . . And maybe you'll review the word tomorrow and maybe you won't. And in either case, it is *okay*. . . . Your child will know there is a word for the concept, even if s/he can't remember what it is. And s/he will know that s/he *understands* the concept, even if s/he can't remember the word. So your child will continue his or her narrative of what s/he learned today: "Well, y'see, this thing—this *cotyledon*—holds the food for the baby plant before it pops out of the soil. . . ."

In my statement of purpose (in the introduction), I say I want to *introduce* vocabulary. Vocabulary isn't too hard. If you use it a few times (and I always use any significant words at least a few times in this book), your children will grasp the central concepts. So what if they forget the words three weeks from today? Or even tonight? If you reintroduce them, they will make the connection once more. They will remember the concept, and the vocabulary will follow. It's that *residual memory* we're looking for, the *concept*, the knowledge that there *is* a word for the concept even if I can't remember it right now. *That's* what we're looking for with our vocabulary. We're *not* looking for college-level mastery.

Far better, it seems to me, for kids to have a nodding acquaintance with scientific concepts and vocabulary than to know nothing at all! Far better that they learn by experience that they can *understand* "strange" words than to believe (through inexperience) that anything unfamiliar is beyond their grasp!

Once they have that initial acquaintance, then next summer, when you visit an aquarium, or next spring, when the flowers begin to bloom, you and your kids can "test" each other (continuing the learning process): "What kind of plant is this? You remember? There were two kinds. One was called *monocot* and the other was *dicot*. Remember? What's the difference between them? Shall we look in the book? . . . What do you think this is: Is it a dicot or a monocot? Does it have netted leaf veins or parallel leaf veins? . . ."

" . . . Well, those are netted leaf veins, but I don't remember whether that's a monocot or a dicot. Can we look it up? . . . "

And so your conversation may continue.

"Okay," you may say, "according to the book, a dicot has netted leaf veins. So if the leaf veins are netted, what kind of root system should we expect? If it's a dicot, what should we expect: a taproot or a fibrous root system? . . ."

Again, your child may remember "nothing," but, actually, s/he will have some sense of familiarity: "We *did* study this! Mom (or Dad) isn't just babbling nonsense! Biologists really *do* use these kinds of characteristics to distinguish between the different types of plants. . . ."

The fact that you can even *talk* about these things—even if your son or daughter doesn't remember the words—places him or her way ahead of his or her peers. S/he has a *mental framework* on which to build.

Your children hardly need to "prove" themselves by achieving a 70- or 80-percent rate of correct answers. But as you use the vocabulary, and as you discuss the concepts, you and your children *will* gain mastery. Maybe not this year. Maybe not next. But *sometime*. And they (and you!) will be years ahead of their classroom-schooled peers.

The point of teaching vocabulary/concepts is to enable your children to see the world in a new way. To notice and pay attention to various attributes of plants and animals that they have never thought about before. To begin to view the world and think the way educated scientists think.

So enjoy yourself, and let your children enjoy themselves. Use the new words *for now*. For the time being. Do the vocabulary drills we recommend. Look at the world around you and find living examples of some of the objects and items and concepts that you are learning. See if your children can identify arachnids or mollusks when you point them out. See if they can explain *why* the animal you are looking at is an arachnid or a mollusk. If not, try to explain it yourself. And that's all.

Occasional real-life reminders throughout the years will prove to you time and again: your children know what they have studied and they are way ahead of their peers.

An Appeal

As with everything else I do, I will be most grateful for any feedback you may give me concerning the contents, format, style or impact of this book!

JOHN HOLZMANN
April 30, 2003

PART 1
INTRODUCTION

INTRODUCTION

The word **biology** means life (*bios*) studies (*logia*) or *the study of living things*. Biologists try to discover all the different living things God has made. They want to know what these living things do when they are alive, why they get sick, and why they die. They try to find out how people might be able to help living things live longer and healthier lives.

Science and the Scientific Method

Biology is a **science**. The word *science* comes from a Latin word that means *knowledge*. But scientific knowledge is not just any kind of knowledge; it is *tested* knowledge. And we get scientific knowledge by using a special method called the *scientific* method.

When scientists use the scientific method,

✦ They very carefully **observe** or look at things;

✦ They **organize** any information (or "data") they find. After a while—after they have made many, many observations, and after they have gathered lots of information,

✦ Make guesses about—or **hypothesize**—*why* they have seen whatever they have seen, and why they have collected the data they have. Finally, once they have made some hypotheses,

✦ They *test* them to see if their hypotheses are right. These tests are called **experiments**.

Before, during, and after their experiments, good scientists do the same things over and over again: they *observe, organize, hypothesize,* and *test*—or *do experiments*.

Finally, after they have done lots and lots of experiments and they are quite sure a hypothesis (or guess!) is correct, scientists will form a *theory*. A **theory** is a hypothesis that, after many, many experimental tests, has always seemed right. It has never been shown wrong.

A Scientist Uses the Scientific Method

Let's suppose a scientist notices—or **observes**—that moths are attracted to a candle flame. All he knows is that every time he lights a candle, moths seem to gather around and flutter near the flame.

The scientist **makes a hypothesis**: The moths aren't attracted to the candle; they are attracted to the flame. And it's not the flame they are attracted to; it is the heat of the flame.

A good scientist then **tests his hypothesis**. This scientist is a good scientist, so he captures the moths, puts them in a room with an electric heater, and turns the heater on. Now he **observes** what happens. The moths don't go any closer to the heater than any other place in the room. He starts to wonder if his idea was wrong.

So he begins to **organize his information** by taking notes. He writes that the moths are attracted to a lighted candle; but they are not attracted to an electric heater.

Now he **makes a new hypothesis**: The moths aren't attracted to heat; they are attracted to light.

He **tests his hypothesis**. He finds a room and makes it dark. He puts a light bulb in the room that will not give off heat, but will glow brightly enough to be seen, but not light the entire room. He turns it on.

He **observes** what happens. Within four seconds, all the moths are fluttering around the light bulb.

He **organizes** his information. He notes that the moths are attracted to the light bulb.

But then he wonders if it is just *these* moths that happen to be attracted to the light bulb? Or will *other* moths be attracted as well? And what if it were a different type of light bulb?

What if it were red light or yellow light rather than white light that came from the light bulb?

So he keeps doing more and more experiments to try to answer his questions. Over time, through continued experiments, careful observation, and organization of his data, the scientist finds exactly what it is that attracts moths to his candle flame, and not just to *his* candle flame, but to all candle flames. Eventually he states a theory: "Moths of the genus _______ are attracted to yellow light, while moths of the genus _______ prefer red light."

Making observations, recording those observations, and organizing those observations, takes up most of a scientist's time. A good scientist doesn't just jump to conclusions without doing a lot of experiments and answering a lot of questions first.

Purpose

Our purpose in this book is to study what scientists called **taxonomists** do. Taxonomists are biologists who look at living things and decide how they are similar and how they are different. When they find a bunch of animals or plants that are similar one to the other, they say they make a group, and then they give that group a name. Taxonomists **observe** and then they **organize** their information.

Besides looking at what taxonomists do, we will also study a few of their **hypotheses** and **theories**.

As we study these things, I hope you will be amazed by God's creativity. This world is full of wonderful living things!

One other very important goal we have is to introduce you to a lot of the words biologists use. If you know their special words, you can understand what they are talking about.

Vocabulary

biology—the study of *living things*

biologist—a person who studies living things

science—tested knowledge

data—information found by careful observation

hypothesis—a guess about what one has observed

theory—an idea that has not been proven 100% true, but, if it is right, would explain some facts or questions.

scientific method—the way scientists test their hypotheses: observe, organize data, form an hypothesis, test the hypothesis through experiments

taxonomist—someone who groups (classifies) and names living things

WHAT THE BIBLE SAYS ABOUT WHERE LIVING THINGS CAME FROM

The Bible says that "God created the heavens and the earth." He created light and separated the light from the darkness. He created land and separated the land from the water. The Bible tells us God said, "Let the land produce vegetation: seed-bearing plants and trees on the land that bear fruit with seed in it, according to their various kinds" (Genesis 1:11). And when God said this, "It was so. The land produced vegetation: plants bearing seed according to their kinds and trees bearing fruit with seed in it according to their kinds" (Genesis 1:12).

After He created the Sun, Moon and stars, God said, "Let the water teem with living creatures, and let birds fly above the earth across the expanse of the sky" (Genesis 1:20). Having said these things, the Bible tells us, God created "the great creatures of the sea and every living and moving thing with which the water teems, according to their kinds, and every winged bird according to its kind" (Genesis 1:21).

Then, we are told, God said, "Let the land produce living creatures according to their kinds: livestock, creatures that move along the ground, and wild animals, each according to its kind" (Genesis 1:24). And again, when God said this, "It was so. God made the wild animals according to their kinds, the livestock according to their kinds, and all the creatures that move along the ground according to their kinds" (Genesis 1:25).

Finally, the Bible tells us, after God had made all the animals, God created human beings—the first man and then the first woman, Adam ("Man") and Eve "the Mother of All Living" (Genesis 3:20).

In Genesis 1:29-30, God tells Adam and Eve, "I give you every seed-bearing plant on the face of the whole earth and every tree that has fruit with seed in it. They will be yours for food. And to all the beasts of the earth and all the birds of the air and all the creatures that move on the ground—everything that has the breath of life in it—I give every green plant for food."

When all of these things were said and done, "God saw all that he had made and it was very good. Thus the heavens and the earth were completed in all their vast array" (Genesis 1:31-2:1).

Having "completed" the heavens and the earth, having "finished the work he had been doing," God rested (Genesis 2:2).

Questions

According to the Bible:

- ✦ Where did living things first come from? Did they just "happen"? *(Living things did not just happen; God created them.)*
- ✦ Did fish develop into snakes or snakes develop into birds? *(No.)* How do you know? *(Because God made each one of them to reproduce "after its own kind.")*
- ✦ Did God create everything all at one time, or was there an order to creation? Were some things made earlier and others later? *(Yes, there was an order. God created some things first and other things later.)*
- ✦ Does it matter to God if fish have babies that are something other than fish or if people have babies that are not human? *(Yes.)* How do you know? *(Because He talks a lot about each "kind" – that each plant, bird, animal, etc. is supposed to reproduce "according to its kind" [Genesis 1:12, 21, 24; see also Genesis 6:20-7:14 and 8:15-19].)*
- ✦ There are several reasons, but what is perhaps the key reason that God created plants with fruits and seeds? *(He made them to be food for us and for "everything that has the breath of life in it" [Gen. 1:29-30].)*
- ✦ According to the Bible, is God still creating new plants or animals? *(No.)* Why do you say that? *(Because the Bible says the heavens and the earth were completed and that God "finished the [creative] work he had been doing.")*

THE BEGINNINGS OF MODERN BIOLOGY

In Genesis Chapter 1, we read that God said all the plants and animals are to reproduce "according to their kind[s]."

Question: What is a "kind"? How can you tell what is one "kind" and what is another? How many different "kinds" of animals and birds and plants are there?

Let's just talk about animals for a minute.

Suppose you were given eight creatures: an ostrich, an eagle, a lobster, an alligator, a snake, a goldfish, a butterfly, and a cheetah. Let's agree to call all of these creatures "animals." Someone asks you: "Are any of these animals like any of the others? If so, please sort them." —What would you say? How would you want to sort them? By color? By size? By whether they have wings or not? . . .

What are the more important differences among these animals? What are least important?

Most people I know would say that the ostrich and the eagle are similar. Would you agree? They are both birds! But one flies and the other does not. Does that mean we should keep them completely separate from each other? Why or why not?

Well, let's assume that the ostrich and the eagle belong together.

Can you see any other animals that should be grouped together? For example, do think the goldfish and the lobster belong together? They both live in water, don't they?

What about the alligator? It lives in water, but it doesn't always stay in water.

And the snake? Its skin has scales like the skin of an alligator. Should we place the snake and the alligator together? Why or why not?

How about the butterfly? It flies. Doesn't that make it a bird? Why or why not?

And the tiger? . . .

All of us like to sort things. But scientists sort animals a little differently from the way you and I might sort them.

In this book, we are going to study many of the plants and animals of the world and see how scientists sort them and try to understand some of the reasons *why* they sort plants and animals as they do.

The Problem of Names

Back in the early 1700s, about 300 years ago, people in different parts of the world had different names for the same plants and animals. Even people who spoke the same language might call the same plant or animal a different name.

Most of the time no one cared that they used different names for the same things. After all, people speak different languages—English, French, Spanish, German, Italian, and so forth—and no one seems to mind.

But there was one group of people for whom different names caused real problems.

Back in the early 1700s, people made medicines from plants, and patients often made the medicines themselves. So imagine how hard it could be to get the right medicine.

Suppose you went to your doctor and he told you to make an ointment from the "foxtail lily." You would look at him blankly. "You know!" he would cry in exasperation: "The foxtail lily! It stands anywhere from three to six feet high and has a bright flower that looks like a bottle-brush . . . ?"

After he described it to you, you might respond, "Oh, you mean the *desert candle*?"

"The desert candle!?" the doctor might exclaim in surprise. "I've never heard of that!" Or, perhaps he would say: "Oh, no! Not the *desert candle*! Why, that's *poisonous*!"

After further discussion—and perhaps a walk out into some gardens nearby—the two of you might realize that when the doctor said "desert candle," he was thinking of something you know as the "wax plant," and when *you* said "desert candle," you were talking about *exactly* the same thing as the doctor meant when he spoke of the "foxtail lily."[1] But since the two of you had different names for the same things, you could never be sure you were talking about the same things.

If only someone could come up with a set of names that people everywhere could use so they would always know what everyone was talking about!

Well, that is exactly what ***Carl von Linné*** (von LIN-ay) decided to do!

Carl von Linné/Carolus Linnaeus

Carl von Linné was born in Sweden in 1707. When he was 28 years old—in 1735—he published a book whose title, in English, means *Systems of Nature*. But von Linné wrote the book in Latin, and since his book was written in Latin, he decided to make his name sound Latin, too. So he called himself ***Carolus Linnaeus*** (CAYR-o-lus lin-NAY-us).

---

[1]Mom or Dad: If you want to look these up on the web, you can find a description of the dangerous variety of desert candle/wax plant under the scientific name *Euphorbia antisyphylitica*. You can find the desert candle/foxtail lily under the scientific name *Eremurus bungei/bungii* and *Eremurus stenophyllus*. To make matters even more interesting, you can also find a "desert candle" under the scientific name *Caulanthus inflatus*.

Nowadays, everyone remembers von Linné by his Latin name: Linnaeus. (Can you say that? *Lin-NAY-us.*)

People think of Linnaeus as one of the "fathers" of modern biology. That's because his book set out the rules by which scientists everywhere name every living thing even today. Linnaeus didn't *name* everything, but he made up the rules by which scientists name things. (We'll talk about those rules in the days to come.)

Scientists who sort and name things are called ***taxonomists*** (tax-ON-oh-mists) and the science of sorting and naming things is called ***taxonomy*** (tax-ON-oh-mee).

Here's how Linnaeus arranged everything.

Linnaeus' System of Taxonomy

Linnaeus sorted all plants—*all* plants—into twenty-four categories. He called those categories "***Classes***."

He made twenty-three classes for plants that produce flowers and one class for all the plants that don't have flowers. Linnaeus sorted the 23 classes of ***flowering plants*** according to how many ***stamens*** they have.[2]

After counting ***stamens***, Linnaeus sorted plants according to the types of ***leaves*** they had (smooth or ragged-edged, thick or thin, hairy or smooth, and so forth), the shape of their flower ***petals***, and on and on. . . .

All of these additional categories Linnaeus called ***Orders***. After the ***Orders*** he split the plants into groups he called ***Genera*** (jen-AIR-uh; more than one ***Genus*** [JEE-nus]). Finally, he split each ***Genus*** into one or more ***Species*** (SPEE-shees).

---

[2]Mom or Dad: We will talk a lot more about stamens later. But if you can find a flower to look at—even a picture of a flower—you will find that, right in the middle, there are some long, thin things poking up. Those long thin things are called ***stamens***. Some plants have only one or two ***stamens***, others have more. Linnaeus used this fact to sort all the different kinds of flowering plants.

Modern Taxonomy

Taxonomists (who are they? *The people who organize and name living things!*) . . . —Taxonomists since Linnaeus' time have added a few more levels to his system. But the modern system is almost exactly the same as the one Linnaeus created.

Consider how modern taxonomists would classify the tiger. The tiger is a member of . . .

- ✦ **Kingdom:** Animal;
- ✦ **Phylum:** Chordate (having a cord of nerves that runs along its back);
- ✦ **Subphylum:** Vertebrate (having vertebrae or backbones that surround the nerve cord);
- ✦ **Class:** Mammalian (having mammary glands that produce milk to feed its young);
- ✦ **Order:** Carnivorous ("meat-eater");
- ✦ **Family:** Felidae (fel-EE-day; *cat*);
- ✦ **Genus:** Panthera (big cat); and
- ✦ **Species:** Panthera tigris (tiger).

You'll notice several things about this method of classification.

1. *All the names are in Latin.*

   Two hundred fifty years ago and before, when Linnaeus did his work, scholars around the world knew and used one language. They all knew Latin. If you wanted other people in other countries to know what you were thinking, you would write your thoughts not in English, German, French, Spanish or Italian; you would write in Latin. People who wanted to write to you, in turn, would write back in Latin as well. That's why Linnaeus wrote his book in Latin. That's also why he changed his name from von Linné to Linnaeus. He wanted all the scientists around the world to be able to read and understand what he was saying.

2. *The genus and species names are normally printed in italics or* underlined; all the other names are printed normally.

3. *Every species has* two *names.*

4. *The first of the two names is like your* last, *or "family," name – it is more general than the second name.*

   If your name were Jason Barrymore, then in Linnaeus' system you really ought to be called Barrymore Jason!

5. *The first species name is the same as the name of the genus.*

6. *The first letter of the first name – the name that is the same as the genus – is always* capitalized; *the first letter of the second name is always printed in lower-case.*

7. *The second name tells you which member of the genus something is. It is like your personal or first name: Sandra, Betty, or Justin.*[3]

8. *The second part of the species name – the "personal" name, if you will – may be used by more than one plant or animal . . . and it can be used by plants and animals!* For instance, there is an Australian fish named the *Yozia tigris*; the big cat-like creature we call a tiger has the same second name. It is called the *Panthera tigris*.

---

[3]Mom or Dad: You may want to stop a moment here and talk about naming conventions. Perhaps you would like to note how Linnaeus' system is like the Chinese naming system: family names come first, personal names come second. Perhaps you would like, also, to have your child practice putting family and personal names in "proper" order according to the standards modern taxonomists use. Thus: is "Don Smith" correct? Or should it be "Smith Don"? How about "Sandra Stone"? Or should it be "Stone Sandra"? How about "Parks Dave"? Or should that be "Dave Parks"? "Randy Taylor" or "Taylor Randy"? . . . (Linnaeus' system *always* puts the Genus name [what would be our English-speaking human "last" or family names] first; the narrower species names – the equivalent to our English-speaking personal names – always come second.) Finally, "just for fun," you might want to write some of the names and have your son or daughter copy them as if they were real plant or animal names: *Smith john; Waters sally; Barnhart cheryl; Adams bill*; and so forth. . . .

9. *While two plants or animals may share the same* second *name, no animals or plants may share the same* two *names.*

   Scientists use special (Latin!) words when talking about this special two-name system. They call it *binomial nomenclature* (BY-no-mee-uhl NO-men-clay-ture). *Bi-* means "two" (as in *bicycle* or *binoculars*). *Nomial* means "name." *Nomenclature* means "naming system." So *binomial nomen-clature* means a "two-name naming system"!

Vocabulary

taxonomy—the practice of sorting and naming things

Carolus Linnaeus—the "father" of modern biology

binomial nomenclature—the standard two-name system of naming living things

Questions

- Besides looking at stamens, what else did Linnaeus look at to determine which class a flower was supposed to belong to? *(The shapes of leaves, flower petals, and so forth.)*
- When scientists talk about a plant's or animal's "class," "order," "phylum," "genus," or "species," what are they really talking about? *(They are talking about the different groups into which they sort them.)*
- When scientists use the system of binomial nomenclature, what *language* do they use? *(Latin.)*
- When using binomial nomenclature, what does a plant's or animal's first name stand for? *(Its **genus**.)* And what does its second name stand for? *(Its **species**.)*

LIVING THINGS

We began our book by saying that ***biology*** *is the study of* ***living things***.

What Is Alive?

What is a living thing? How do we know if something is alive? That seems like a silly question, doesn't it? You can tell if cats and dogs and birds are alive by whether they are breathing and their hearts are beating, right? If they move, they are alive.

But what about plants? Are they alive? Do they breathe? Do they have heartbeats? (Actually, plants do breathe. But they don't have hearts and they don't have lungs.)

So how does a biologist know if something is alive?

When we look at some things, like very, very tiny bacteria ("germs"), it's hard to know!

Still, biologists say there are several good clues to look for to tell if something is alive.

Clues that Tell You if Something Is Alive

1. *All living things include* **four chemicals**: *carbon, hydrogen, oxygen, and nitrogen.*[1] Although plants and animals include many other chemicals as well, they are mostly made up of these four.

---

[1]Chemicals are types of matter. *Carbon* is the material from which charcoal, pencil "lead," and diamonds are made. *Hydrogen, oxygen,* and *nitrogen* are all included in the air you breathe.

2. *Living things are made of* ***cells***. Cells are the basic building blocks of all living things.[2] Most cells are very small, and you can't see them without looking through a microscope. The diagram at right shows what a group of plant cells might look like under a microscope. All cells have at least three parts. They have information-centers called ***nuclei*** (NOO-klee-igh; singular: nucleus [NOO-klee-us]; the black bean-shaped blobs in the center of each cell in the picture); they have cell membranes that surround the cell; and they have a liquid or jelly-like material inside the walls and surrounding the nuclei called ***cytoplasm*** (SIGH-toe-plazm; the gray parts of the picture).

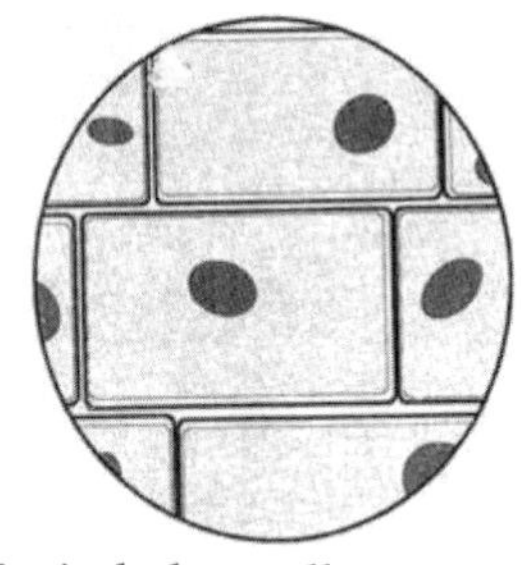

Typical plant cells.

3. *All living things* ***use energy***. It is true that non-living things can store and release energy. (A rock, for instance, can become hot by storing energy from the Sun's light and then slowly release that energy during the night.) But living things use energy to grow and perhaps to move around.

4. *All living things use* ***food*** *to get energy.*[3]

---

[2]Of course, living things are also made of atoms and molecules, but living things have this higher level design structure called the cell. Non-living things have none of the cellular structure we find in living things.

[3]Scientists have a special word for the process by which living things change food into the energy they need. The process is called ***metabolism***. Metabolism includes eating food, digesting it, moving the digested food into the cells; releasing the energy contained in the food, and excreting, or getting rid of, whatever waste materials are left over.

We can't describe the whole process here, but one thing you should know: plants' and animals' cells use oxygen to release the energy in their food.

5. Living things ***reproduce***—they have children. Not only do plants and animals themselves reproduce. The cells *within* plants and animals also reproduce. (By contrast, non-living things—rocks, for instance—don't have babies.) All living things come from other living things.

6. All living things tend to ***grow***.

7. Each type of living thing has a ***normal form and size***. Every different type of frog, for instance, tends to grow only so large. And each type of frog is always shaped in more or less the same way. Non-living things, by contrast, can have different shapes and they can come in almost any size. Think of a rock. Rocks can be of almost any shape or size. Sizes can range from so small you can't see them, to the size of a mountain.

8. Living things are ***irritable***. That doesn't mean that living things are grouchy. When scientists say living things are irritable, that means they *react* to changes in their environment. For example, plants open and close special holes in their leaves, depending on how much water is in the air, how hot it is, and how bright the sun is. Dogs often shed their fur in the springtime and grow heavier coats in the fall. Sea anemones pull in their tentacles whenever anything touches them.

Vocabulary

cells—the basic building blocks of life; they are composed, among other things, of ***nuclei***, ***walls***, and ***cytoplasm***

nucleus/nuclei—the information center(s) of a cell

cytoplasm—the liquid or jelly-like substance that fills a cell

irritable—able to respond to the environment

energy—what enables living things to move, grow, keep warm, etc.

chemicals (optional) — the basic building blocks of the physical world; chemicals are made of atoms

reproduce — to have children, to generate offspring

metabolism (optional) — the process by which food is digested, food energy is released, and waste products are excreted

Questions

- ✦ Which feature of living things does each of the following examples illustrate? Eating toast for breakfast *(living things use food to get energy; this is called **metabolism**)*; yelling "ouch" when you touch a hot stove *(irritability)*; corn seeds that you plant in the spring wind up having stalks that are as tall as you are *(growth)*.
- ✦ Where do living things come from? *(ultimately, from God; but, from a scientific perspective, they **reproduce**)*

SOME OTHER OBSERVATIONS ABOUT LIVING THINGS[1]

1. Everything in the universe is made of atoms and molecules. Atoms and molecules are not alive, but they follow the rules that God has made for them. ***The cells of plants and animals use and follow the rules God made for atoms and molecules.*** For instance, God has made certain rules that tell atoms when and how they can link up with other atoms and when and how they have to stay away from each other. Our bodies use these rules to help us metabolize our food and to breathe.

2. Wherever a plant or animal lives is called its ***habitat***. (*Habitat* means "home.") Some habitats are hot and dry; others are cold and wet. Some places are rocky, others are sandy. . . . ***Living things are usually well-suited*** (scientists say they are "*well-adapted*") ***to their habitats***. They have what they need to survive in the places they live. That's why, for instance, you don't find fish living in the desert, and you don't find mice living near the North Pole!

3. ***Living things come from living things.*** Living things don't come from non-living things (like rocks, or from out of the air). Scientists call this the law of ***biogenesis*** (BI-oh-JEN-uh-sis; *bios* = life; *genesis* = beginning).[2]

---

[1]Mom or Dad: Take your time and enjoy the *wonder* of what we're talking about here. Don't worry if your child doesn't "get" everything or remember all—or even most—of the details. Our purpose here is merely to *expose* your child to these ideas and to let you—the two of you—enjoy the wonders of God's creation. These things really are amazing.

[2]Strangely, though no one has ever observed *abiogenesis* (AY-bi-oh-jen-uh-sis; beginning from *non*-life), most modern biologists seem to think that, with no help from God, all the living things in the world today "just started" (they say, "evolved") from non-living things—from chemicals that were floating around in water!

4. We said that the cell's ***nucleus*** is an information-center. It stores all the design information not only for the cell, but for the living thing—the organism—of which the cell is a part. It stores this information in chemical threads called ***genes***. Each gene is like a word in a book. It tells one thing about the organism.

   For example, the cells in your body have genes that tell your body whether it is supposed to have green, blue, black or brown eyes. Other genes tell your body exactly what skin color and hair color you are supposed to have, the shape of your nose . . . —everything about you. It is the genes in your cells that make you look a little bit like your mom and a little bit like your dad.

   Without genes, there would be no such things as cells. At best, you might find piles of the kind of "stuff" of which cells are made. Kind of like piles of rocks: if you have a plan, and the brains and tools to move the rocks to follow the plan, then you can build a nice house. But without a plan—a design—even if you have tools and brains, you'll never find anything more than a pile of rocks.

   So it is with living things. When God said each living thing was supposed to reproduce "after its kind," He put all the instructions about *how* to "reproduce after their kinds" into the genes of the living things.

5. Remember that the genes are chemical threads. Every gene is made up of hundreds, and usually thousands of chemical "letters." The chemicals are all strung together, and, depending on what order you find them, they say different things.

   The gene "words," then, are strung together in longer threads called ***chromosomes***. Each chromosome is like a big book.

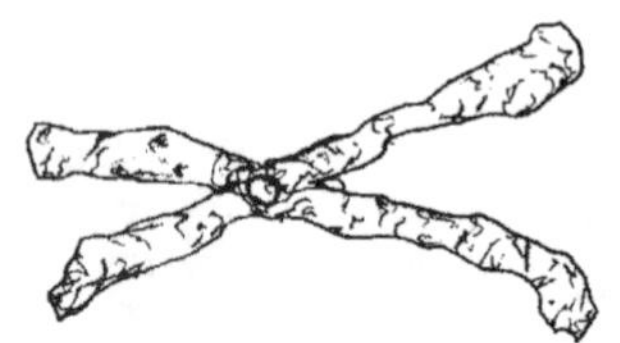

One human chromosome. Each arm of the chromosome has hundreds of genes in it.

Human cells—the cells in your body—have 46 chromosome "books." Scientists don't know yet, but they guess that those 46 chromosome "books" include somewhere between 30,000 and 150,000 gene "words." This book—the one you hold in your hands—has about 30,000 words in it. But this book is very short compared to the genetic books inside your cells.

This book has only about 150,000 letters in it—about five letters per word. All the gene "words" in your body, together, contain about *three billion* (3,000,000,000) chemical letters—somewhere between 20,000 and 100,000 letters per "word"!

If the chemical letters in your cells were as big as the letters on this page, instead of reading five-letter words that are about a third of an inch long each, you could be reading words that are 100,000 letters long and that stretch a tenth of a mile—almost the length of two football fields![3] Each gene *word* would be that long! And your cells contain 30,000 to maybe even 150,000 of those words in them![4]

---

[3]That's how long the average gene would be if you had "only" 30,000 genes! If you had 150,000 genes, then the average gene would be "only" 20,000 letters long and, if the letters were the same size as the letters on this page, would stretch "only" 110 feet—one and a half times the length of a normal lap-length swimming pool!

[4]Scientists are doing a lot of studies right now about genes and what they call *genomes* (the full series of genes for living organisms). Viruses—which are "kind of" alive, but rely on the genes of other organisms to reproduce—have the very shortest genomes. So far, the shortest genome anyone has discovered is just over 5,000 chemical letters long; that is for the virus Phi-X 174. After viruses, the next shortest genomes belong to bacteria. The *Mycoplasma genitalium* bacterium has 517 genes made up of just over 580,000 letters. In 2002, scientists discovered another living organism, *Nanoarchaeum equitans,* that they figure has between 200 and 300 genes.

Here's something that has scientists stumped. Amphibians—things like toads and salamanders—often have more genetic information than humans do! Some amphibians may have 100 times as much genetic information as we do! Biologists can't figure out why simple creatures like amphibians need so much more genetic information than creatures like human beings do.

6. ***Living things that have more than one cell have different kinds of cells.*** For instance, in your body, your skin cells are different from your muscle cells; your muscle cells are different from your bone cells; your bone cells are different from your blood cells; your blood cells are different from your nerve cells; your nerve cells are different from your hair cells; and so forth.
7. ***Though a living creature's cells are different, the genetic information in all of its cells is the same.*** The genetic information in every one of your cells is exactly the same as the genetic information in every other one of your cells. Because each cell has the same genetic information and the genetic information is contained in each cell's nucleus, scientists call this the *principle of* ***nuclear equivalence.***
8. ***All living things inherit their genes—and, therefore, their genetic information—from their parents' cells.*** When cells reproduce, they don't have babies; instead, they split in two. All of the genetic information goes to both of the new cells. God has made a special mechanism so that when plants and animals reproduce, their babies receive half of their genetic information from their fathers and half of their genetic information from their mothers. That's why children usually look a bit like their fathers *and also* a bit like their mothers.
9. ***Every type of plant and animal has a normal life cycle.*** All the members of each of these groups tend to begin in the same way, tend to grow in a particular pattern, tend to mature at about the same time and in the same way. They all show the same kinds of symptoms of growing old, and they all tend to die in much the same way as all the other members of their group do.
10. ***The cells in multi-cellular (more than one cell) plants and animals communicate with and affect each other.*** This is related to the fact that living things are irritable.

Vocabulary

habitat—home, the place where an organism lives, its environment

biogenesis—the beginning of life from life

abiogenesis—the idea (never seen) that life can come from something that is not alive

genes—chemical threads that are in the nuclei of all cells; they contain all the design information the cells need to live and reproduce; they also control how a living organism will look and act

chromosomes—chemical threads made up of lots of genes; if genes are like genetic "words," then chromosomes are like genetic "books"

nuclear equivalence—the fact that all the cells in a body, even though the cells themselves are different, contain exactly the same genetic information

Questions

✦ Name at least two of the four chemicals you will find in every living thing. *(nitrogen, hydrogen, oxygen, carbon)*

✦ What does a scientist mean when s/he says "living things are well-adapted to their habitats"? *(They have design features that make it relatively easy for them to survive wherever they tend to live.)*

✦ How many chromosomes are there in human cells? *(46)* About how many genes are in those chromosomes? *(somewhere between 30,000 and 150,000)* About how many chemical "letters" are there in the human genome (i.e., in the nucleus of every human cell)? *(about 3 billion!)* If the letters in your genes were as big as the letters on this page, about how long would each gene be? *(somewhere between one and a half times the length of a standard lap-lane swimming pool and almost two lengths of a football field!)*

PART 2
CLASSIFICATION

THE TWO MAIN KINGDOMS: PLANTS AND ANIMALS

Traditionally, biologists have divided their studies into two parts called ***kingdoms***. They call one the ***plant kingdom*** and the other the ***animal kingdom***.[1]

The study of plants is called ***botany*** (BAW-tuh-nee).

The study of animals is called ***zoology*** (zoh-AWL-uh-jee).

You know what plants are, right? Plants are living things that have roots and leaves and stay in one place. They get their nourishment from the soil, the air and the water that surround them.

Animals are pretty easy to identify, too, aren't they? They move around. They don't have roots or leaves. And they eat their food. . . . Or do they?

In the late 1500s and early 1600s, scientists began making microscopes. As they looked through their microscopes, they began to find that there were living things that were only one cell big. Were these things plants? Were they animals? Were they something else?

They were (and are) a lot different from the larger plants and animals we can see without microscopes! These little things don't have roots or leaves. Not all of them move around. Some of them get their nourishment from their environment, but others seem to eat. . . . So what are they? Are they plants? Are they animals?

Not only did biologists begin finding these microscopic creatures; they began finding more and more big plants and animals that seemed to break the rules. There were things that seemed, without doubt, to be plants—but they ate insects!

---

[1]There are other groups of living things (such as fungi [FUN-jigh], bacteria, and algae [AL-jee]) that do not belong to either the animal or plant kingdoms. Biologists differ in the way they classify these organisms. We talk about some of these organisms at the end of this book.

(Plants don't eat things, do they? Only animals do that . . . right? Or am I wrong? . . . Keep reading and find out!) And then there were other things—corals and sponges for instance—that *looked* like plants, but, on closer inspection, didn't seem like plants at all! So what were they? Were they animals? Or were they something else?

As biologists looked at more and more living things, they found it harder and harder to say what, exactly, a plant is, and what, exactly, an animal is.[2]

How Can You Tell the Difference Between Plants and Animals?

Over the years, scientists have found at least three things that set animals apart from plants.

Shape and Structure

Plant bodies are different from animal bodies. The same species of tree might have five branches when it is young, but have five hundred branches when it is old; it may have seventy-nine leaves when it is young, but five thousand leaves when it is older. Animal bodies will grow as they get older, but most animals' bodies stay pretty much the same throughout their lives. Baby elephants and old elephants always have four legs, one head, one trunk, two eyes, etc.

Moreover, plant cells are different from animal cells. One big way they differ: plant cell walls are usually hard ("woody"); animal cell walls are usually soft and flexible.

---

[2]This is something you will find as you grow older. Many times people who don't know much about a subject will be very sure they know exactly what is true. People who know more about the subject are less sure. The people who really know what they are talking about will sometimes seem the least sure. You will often hear them say, "It's not that simple! . . . "

How They Get Energy

Plants have special food factories in their leaves called ***chloroplasts*** (CLORE-oh-plasts). These ***chloroplasts*** have a special chemical in them called chlorophyll (CLORE-uh-fill). ***Chlorophyll*** allows plants to use energy from the Sun to turn chemicals in the soil and the air into food! This food-making process is called ***photosynthesis*** or "making by light" (*photo* means "light"; *synthesis* means "making").

Animals cannot make their own food. They must either eat food that plants make, or else they must eat other animals that have eaten plants.[3]

Irritability

Plants and animals are both irritable, but plants respond rather slowly to changes around them. Most animals have nervous systems that help them respond quickly to changes.[4]

---

[3]God has made plants and animals to provide other things for one another. For example, when they make their food, plants break apart oxygen and carbon atoms that have been "glued" together in a gas called carbon dioxide. When they make their food, plants always wind up with a few oxygen atoms left over. Plants let some of these oxygen atoms go out into the air where animals can breathe them. (Even though each plant releases only a little oxygen, since there are so many plants, there is plenty of oxygen in the air for animals to breathe.)

Well, now, guess what the animals do? They breathe in the oxygen and use it to ***metabolize*** their food (release the energy stored in the food) so their bodies can stay warm, move, grow and reproduce. When animals digest their food, their bodies take some of the oxygen atoms they have breathed in and "glue" them to some of the carbon atoms that are in their food. When "glued" together, these carbon and oxygen atoms form the gas called carbon dioxide! And when animals breathe out, they release this carbon dioxide into the air. Can you guess what happens to the carbon dioxide once it's in the air? Yes! Plants use it to make food! (Remember where the cycle started?)

Plants and animals help each other in other ways, too, but we won't talk about those things right now.

[4]Some animals, such as sponges, do not have nervous systems.

Vocabulary

zoology – the study of animals

botany – the study of plants

photosynthesis – making by light: the process by which plants make food for themselves; they use sunlight to put basic chemicals to make food

chlorophyll (optional) – the chemical compound that allows plants to use sunlight to make food

chloroplast (optional) – the part of plant leaves in which you find ***chlorophyll*** and in which photosynthesis takes place

Questions

- ✦ What are the two largest kingdoms of living things? *(**Animals** and **plants**.)*
- ✦ Describe two of the four main differences between plants and animals. *(Answer may include **form** and **size** [plants, in general, while they grow in size, also become more complex; animals will grow in size, but their basic form doesn't usually change]; **cells** [plant cells have hard {"woody"} cell walls; animal cells have soft cell walls]; **food source** [plants generate their own food; animals rely on plants – or other animals that have eaten plants – as their source of food]; and **nervous system** [plants have no nervous system, so they respond to external stimuli very slowly; animals respond quickly].)*
- ✦ Where do plants get their energy? *(From food they manufacture by means of **photosynthesis**.)* Where do animals get their energy? *(From plants or from other animals that have eaten plants.)*

THE PLANT KINGDOM

In Genesis 1, God says He made the seed- and fruit-bearing plants and the trees to serve as food for "everything that has the breath of life in it" (Genesis 1:30).

Biology shows us how true this is. Seed- and fruit- bearing plants are the primary source of food for every animal on earth. Green plants use energy from the Sun to help them make sugars and starches—the basic food for all living things.

While plants make food, they also do something else that provides something "everything that has the breath of life in it" needs. Plants grab carbon dioxide molecules out of the air. Each carbon dioxide molecule has one carbon atom and two oxygen atoms in it. Plants use the carbon atoms and some of the oxygen atoms to make sugar. All the "extra" oxygen that they don't need to make sugar, they put back into the air. Animals need the oxygen to be able to breathe. So the plants give us the oxygen we need![1]

So if God hadn't created plants, there wouldn't be any animals or people, either, because we wouldn't have any food to eat and we wouldn't have enough oxygen to breathe.

The Vascular Plants

Botanists figure that there are about 300,000 different species of plants in the world. They place most of these plants in one ***phylum***.[2] They are called ***vascular***[3] *plants* because of the

[1]Plants "breathe" oxygen, too. They don't have lungs, but their cells use oxygen to metabolize the food they need in order to live! Even after the plants have made sugars and starches; and even after they have metabolized those sugars and starches to keep themselves alive, they still give off more oxygen than they use—so animals have oxygen to breathe.

way they are made. They have circulation systems just like the blood circulation systems in our bodies. But instead of blood, the vessels in plants carry ***sap***.

All plants except mosses and liverworts are ***vascular plants***.

The Parts of Vascular Plants

The bodies of vascular plants have three main parts: ***stems***, ***leaves***, and ***roots***. Inside the stems, leaves and roots are the ***sap vessels***.

In our bodies, blood carries nutrients (that come from our intestines), and oxygen (from our lungs) out to all the cells. After it has delivered these nutrients and oxygen *to* the cells, our blood then picks up any wastes our cells have produced – things like carbon dioxide and nitrogen – and brings them *from* our cells *to* our kidneys, livers, and lungs. Our kidneys, livers and lungs then strain these wastes out of our blood and ***excrete*** them (get rid of them).

As we've said, vascular plants have sap instead of blood. And instead of blood vessels, they have vessels that carry sap. The vessels carry the sap from the tips of their roots to the outer edges of their leaves(1). The sap carries water and nutrients up from the soil into all the different cells(1); and it moves the food that the plant produces in its leaves from the leaves to the all of the rest of the cells throughout the plant (2).

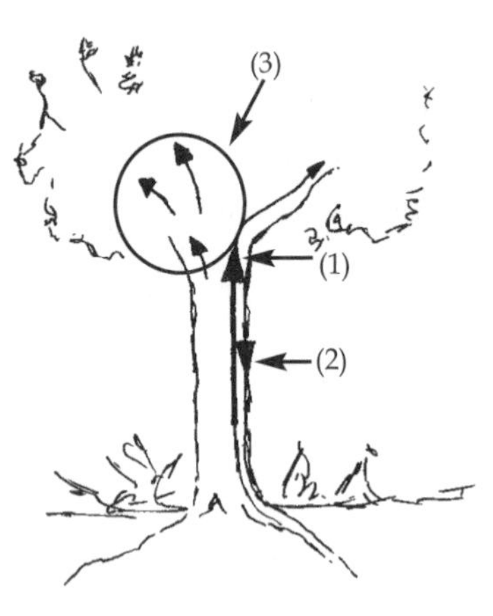

[2]Remember: all living things are organized according to **kingdom**, **phylum**, **class**, **order**, **family**, **genus** and **species**.

[3]*Vascular* is from the Latin word *vas* which means *vessel* – having vessels: like your blood vessels. Another word we could use for *vessel* (at least when talking about plants and animals) is *pipe*. You have blood pipes in your body; plants have sap pipes.

A plant's cells use the food that they get from the leaves to stay alive and to grow. As they use this food, the plant cells also produce wastes (in fact, the same wastes that animal cells produce: carbon dioxide and nitrogen). But there is a difference. While animals have no use for carbon dioxide and nitrogen and must excrete them from their bodies, plants' ***chloroplasts***[4] need so much carbon dioxide and nitrogen in order to make food that even though they bring in carbon dioxide and nitrogen from the soil and the air, they also use up all the wastes (the carbon dioxide and nitrogen) that their own cells produce (3).

Xylem and Phloem

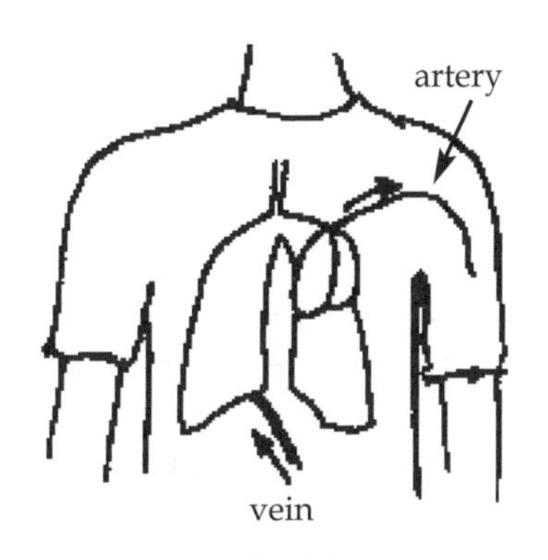

Our bodies have two types of blood vessels, ***veins***, and ***arteries***. The **arteries** carry blood from our hearts and lungs out to all the cells of our bodies. The blood in our arteries is filled with oxygen and nutrients. Our blood **veins**, by contrast, carry blood from our cells back to our hearts and lungs. The blood in our veins has very little oxygen and few nutrients. But it is filled with carbon dioxide and other wastes produced by our cells.

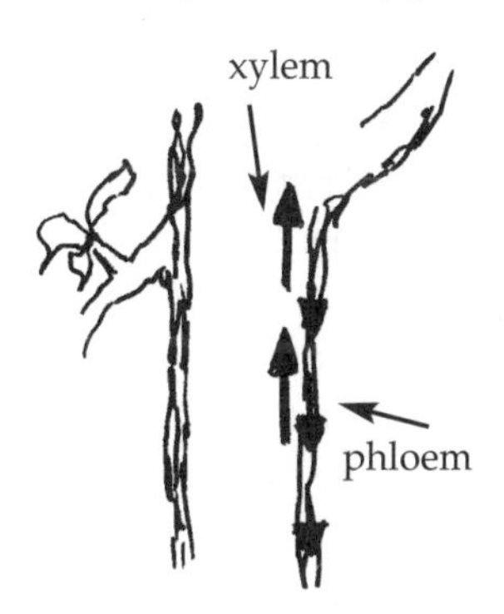

In the same way that our bodies have arteries and veins to carry nutrients one way and wastes the other, so vascular plants have two types of vessels as well. They have ***xylem*** (ZY-lem) and ***phloem*** (FLOH-um). The **xylem** is like our arteries; it carries nutrients

[4]Remember: Chloroplasts are the places where chlorophyll uses the energy of the Sun to change carbon dioxide, water and nitrogen into food!

and water from the soil up from the roots, through the stems, out the branches, to the tips of the leaves. The **phloem** is like our blood veins in that it carries the food that the leaves produce back down the leaves, down the branches, down the stem, and back to the roots. All along the way, if some cells need food, they take what they need.

There is a helpful device for remembering the difference between the xylem and the phloem: remember that phloem, which sounds like "flow," allows the sap to *flow* downhill back to the roots. Xylem, of course, carries the fluids *up*.

In small plants, it is hard to tell the difference between xylem and phloem: they are mixed together. In trees and woody plants, however, they are separated. The xylem is on the outside edge of the woody portion, and the phloem is on the inside edge of the bark.

Laboratory Exercises

- Take a look at the xylem and phloem in a small branch or twig from a tree. Perhaps you can slice the twig lengthwise so you can see the twig's structure from the side. Notice that the lines are all lengthwise. The xylem is in the center, green or yellow portion of the stem; the phloem is just under the outside skin or bark. Can you separate some of the vascular fibers?

- Celery has an extremely easy-to-see vascular system. Take a stalk of celery that still has some leaves attached to it, and cut off the bottom ½ inch (1 cm). Place it right side up in a glass that has a few inches (about 6 cm) of water with some red food coloring added to it. Leave it there for a day or two. You will notice that the xylem carries the water, with the red food coloring, up the stalk into the leaves. People who sell flowers use this idea to make white flowers (especially carnations) turn all different colors. Now you can cut the celery stalk crosswise, and see the arrangement of the xylem in the stem.

Vocabulary

vascular—having vessels or tubes

sap—the "blood" of plants; the liquid that transports nutrients and waste materials throughout a plant

arteries— the blood vessels that carry blood from our hearts and lungs out to all the cells of our bodies

veins—the blood vessels that transport blood from the cells back to the heart and lungs

xylem—the vessels that transport nutrients and water from the soil up through a plant's roots and stems to its leaves

phloem—the vessels that transport food wherever it is needed in a plant—from its leaves back down through the stems and to the roots

Questions

- ✦ What are the three main parts of vascular plants? *(stems, leaves, roots)*
- ✦ What do a plant's leaves do? *(They produce food for the plant.)*
- ✦ What do a plant's roots do? *(They absorb nutrients and water from the soil; they also support the plant and keep it from falling over.)*
- ✦ What do a plant's stems do? *(They provide the main structure of the plant and support the leaves, the xylem, and the phloem.)*
- ✦ What do the xylem and the phloem do? *(The xylem transports nutrients and water up from the roots to the leaves; the phloem transports the food produced in a plant's leaves back down from the leaves to all the cells along the way all the way down to the roots.)*
- ✦ Where will you find the xylem: on the outside of the woody portion of a tree, or the inside of the bark? *(On the outside of the woody portion.)*
- ✦ Why do you think it will kill a tree if you "girdle" it (i.e., cut a complete ring of bark off of its trunk)?

The Spermatophytes

Botanists split the Vascular Plants into five groups that they call "divisions," "classes," or "subphyla":[5]

1. ***Spermatophytes*** (sper-MA-toe-fites; literally: seed plants; *sperm* = seed; *phytes* = plants). There are about 250,000 species of seed plants.
2. ***Pteridophytes*** (tare-ID-oh-fites; literally: wing plants; *pteri* = wing). The *pteridophytes* include all the ferns. Fern leaves look a bit like wings! There are about 9,500 species of *pteridophytes*.
3. ***Lycophytes*** (literally: wolf plants; *lycos* = wolf). It appears that there may be about 1,000 species of *lycophytes* in the world today.[6]
4. ***Psilophytes*** (SY-low-fites; literally: barren plants; a special type of plant that has no leaves). There are possibly eight species of *psilophytes*.[7]
5. ***Sphenophytes*** ("horsetails"). There are about fifteen species of *sphenophytes* still in existence.[8]

Since the spermatophytes or seed-bearers have so many more species than any of the others, we'll just talk about them.

The spermatophytes are divided into two "classes"

1. ***Angiosperms*** ("covered seeds"); and
2. ***Gymnosperms*** ("naked seeds").

---

[5]Different authors use different names for these groups. For all practical purposes, it doesn't matter what you call them. The groups themselves go by the same names whether they are "divisions," "classes," or "subphyla."

[6]You can find photos of the *lycophytes* at www.science.siu.edu/landplants/Lycophyta/lycophyta.html.

[7]Photos of a few *psilophytes* may be found at www.science.siu.edu/landplants/Psilophyta/psilophyta.html

[8]See www.science.siu.edu/landplants/Sphenophyta/sphenophyta.html for photos.

Angiosperms include all the flowering and fruiting plants. There are about 250,000 species of angiosperms. The *gymnosperms* are mostly ***conifers*** (cone-bearing trees like pines and evergreens). There are only about 550 species of gymnosperms.

Angiosperms are called *angiosperms* ("covered seeds") because when their seeds mature, they are covered—either by a protective pod or by fruit. Can you think of anything you eat that comes in a pod? (How about peas, or beans? —Those are *angiosperms*, because the peas and beans are the seeds. And the seeds are covered.)

Examples of gymnosperms include pines, furs, junipers, and other needle-leafed evergreens.

The seeds of *gymnosperm* ("naked seed") plants develop in a seed cone (such as a pine cone). When they are mature, these cones open up and the seeds fall to the ground by themselves. They don't fall while they are still inside a pod or a piece of fruit. They fall to the ground "naked." And so they are called ***gymnosperms*** ("naked seeds"). Gymnosperms do not produce flowers and they don't produce fruit.

Laboratory Exercise

Look at the seeds in a piece of fruit or a vegetable (such as green beans, cucumbers, or squash). If you can locate a pine-cone that hasn't been open too long, perhaps you can find some seeds still inside of that, too. Can you see why the one kind of seed is said to be "covered" while the other is "naked"?

Vocabulary

sperm—seed

phyte—plant

ptero-/pteri-[9] — wing

angiosperm — covered seed

gymnosperm — naked seed

conifer — having cones

Questions

- How do you tell the difference between an ***angiosperm*** and a ***gymnosperm***? *(An **angiosperm**'s seeds are "covered": they come inside **fruit** or **pods**; **gymnosperm** seeds, by contrast, usually grow inside cones that open and let the seeds fall onto the ground by themselves ["naked"].)*
- When God said that He had made all the seed- and fruit-bearing trees and plants for food, was He talking about ***angiosperms*** or ***gymnosperms***? How can you tell? *(He must have been talking about both angiosperms and gymnosperms because, though the gymnosperms have no fruits, they do have seeds! Angiosperms, of course, have both fruits and seeds.)*

---

[9]You may wonder why we emphasize this prefix. We do so because you will run across it later in this book; you will also run across it in future years. For instance, it is part of the name of the *archaeo**pteryx*** (the supposed "first bird") and the ***ptero**dactyl* (a huge, bat-like reptile that lived long ago).

FLOWERS

What They Do

Flowers are the parts of plants that form seeds and allow plants to **reproduce**, or have babies.

Flower Parts

Angiosperm flowers come in all shapes and sizes. But almost all angiosperm flowers have four main parts. Starting from the base of the flower and working upward, most flowers have a **calyx** (CAL-ix) made of **sepals** (SEE-puls); a **corolla** (cu-ROLE-uh) which is made up of **petals**; one or more—usually many more—**stamens** (STAY-mens) and/or (instead of stamens) one or more—usually several—**pistils** (PISS-t'ls).[1]

The Calyx and Sepals

Look at the diagram of a flower on page 42. Notice the "leaves" at the base of the flower that bend down toward the stem. These "leaves" are called **sepals**. In many flowers the sepals are green, but in some flowers the sepals look like petals. In fact, you can't tell the difference between them.[2]

The sepals are the first part of the flower to grow. They form a protective coat, called the **calyx**, for the rest of the flower as it first starts to grow. If you look at a rose bud or a tulip flower before it opens, the outside of that bud is made of

---

[1]We said *most* flowers have these parts because there are a few plants that have two different types of flowers, one that includes stamens but not pistils, and the other that includes pistils but not stamens. Once you know what the stamens and pistils do, you will know why some flowers can have both and others can get away with only one or the other.

[2]Irises, lilies, and orchids have sepals that look like petals.

sepals, and that is what is called the calyx. The calyx is the part of the bud that you can see. So the sepals make the calyx, and the calyx forms the outer shell of the flower bud that protects the flower until it is big enough to come out and be affected by the sunshine, rain, and weather.

Once the other parts of the flower have gotten big enough, they burst out of the calyx. The calyx, then, simply sits below the rest of the flower.

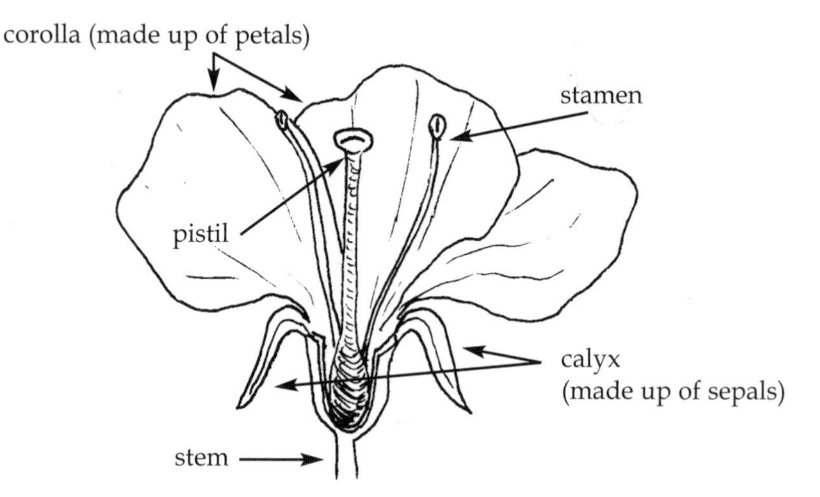

The Corolla and Petals

The **corolla** is what most of us think of when we think of a flower: it is made up of the flower's **petals**. It is the biggest, brightest, and, usually, the most fragrant part of the flower. The colors and odors of the corolla attract insects or birds to the flower. And God designed the corolla to attract insects and birds to flowers so they can help the flowers reproduce.

Stamens and Pistils

God made plants and animals in a very special way.

With only a few exceptions, He made it so that there can be no baby plants and no baby animals unless there is both a mother and a father plant or animal.

Before we say any more about how plants make babies, we need to understand two things.

1. God designed everything He made. He didn't just toss some chemicals together, shake them up, and say, "Hey! That will work!" He *designed* everything very carefully.
2. God's design for living things is *stored in every living cell.*

You may recall that every cell has an information center called a nucleus.[3] The nuclei of cells contain at least two kinds of information. First, they contain all the *operational* information they need to *stay alive*. Second, they contain all the *design* information they need to *reproduce*. You could say the nucleus contains the "blueprints" for new cells. The eye cells have all the information they need in order to produce more eye cells. Skin cells have all the information they need to produce new skin cells. Bone cells have all the information they need to produce more bone cells, and so on. All the different cells have all the information they need to produce cells just like themselves.

But where does the design information come from that tells all these cells have to grow and produce a *whole body*? What tells all the different cells in a plant to grow so that they produce a plant and not, say, a huge stem, tiny leaves, and almost no roots?

What tells a plant that it needs 2,496,000 cells of one type and 135,398,000 cells of another type? (A plant would look pretty strange if it produced too many leaf cells and not enough stem cells, don't you think?)

Well, besides the regular cells that make up plant and animal and human bodies (the leaf and stem and root cells, the claw and tooth and skin cells, and all the other kinds of cells), God designed special reproductive cells called **gametes**. Gametes tell organisms—plants and animals, all living things—how to produce more living things just like themselves.

Sparrow gametes contain all the design information required to make baby sparrows. Possum gametes contain all the information

---

[3]See page 18.

to make baby possums. Corn gametes include all the information to make baby corn plants, and oak gametes include all the information to make baby oak trees, etc.

Except there is one more part to the puzzle.

Each *single* gamete only has *half* the information necessary to make a baby. You need *two* gametes—one from a male and one from a female—in order to have all the information necessary to make a baby.

That's why there has to be a father and a mother in order to make a baby. Every baby bird has to have a father and a mother bird. Every baby chipmunk has to have a father and a mother chipmunk. And every baby plant that grows from a seed also has to have a father and a mother plant.

In angiosperms, the **stamens** are the male or "father" parts and the **pistils** are the female or "mother" parts. They work together to make seeds.

Stamens—Plants' Male Organs

Stamens have two main parts: a **filament** and an **anther**. The filament is the base for the anther, and the anther makes **pollen**.

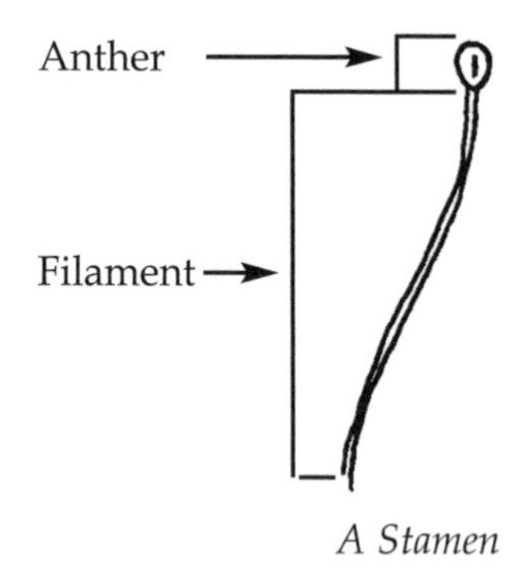

A Stamen

Each grain of pollen contains two *male* gametes called **sperms**. Even though the anther produces lots of pollen, and even though each grain of pollen has two sperms, the sperms cannot form baby plants until they are combined with *female* gametes from the same species.

How do the sperms get together with *female* gametes so they can form baby plants? Here's what happens.

The anther holds the pollen until the pollen is ripe—in other words, until it is ready to make babies. Once the pollen is ripe, the anther bursts open and releases the pollen into the air to be blown around by the wind—or to be carried by birds and bees.

So where does it go? We'll get to that in a minute.

Pistils—Plants' Female Organs

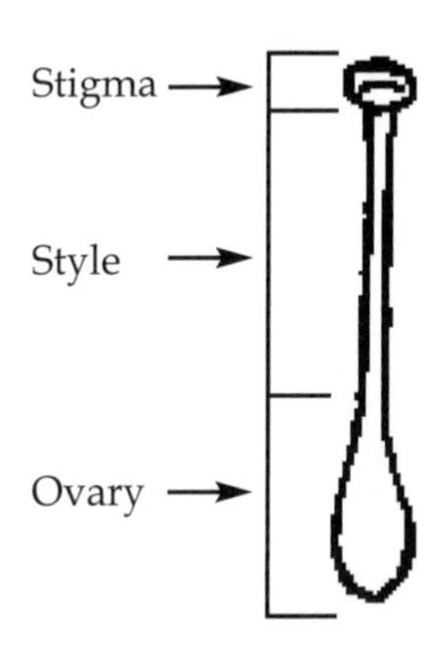

A Pistil

Pistils have three parts: a stigma, a style, and an ovary. The **ovary** sits at the base of the pistil. It is where ovules are made. **Ovules** are *female* plant gametes.

Above the ovary is the style. The **style** is a tube that connects the ovary to the stigma.

The **stigma** is at the top of the pistil. It has a sticky surface. Its purpose is to catch grains of pollen.

Pollination & Fertilization

Scientists say that **pollination** takes place when pollen from a certain species of plant is moved from the **anther** of such a plant to the **stigma** of such a plant. When a stigma catches pollen, scientists say the plant has been pollinated.

What causes pollen to move from an anther to a stigma? For some plants, especially when they are planted close together, the wind blows each plant's pollen around until it gets caught by one of its "next door neighbors." Corn is usually pollinated in this way. That's why corn is usually planted in large fields: so the stigmas on each corn plant have plenty of opportunities to catch pollen from their neighbors.

Some trees and most wild grasses pollinate themselves the same way.

Other plants need some help to get pollinated. For them, wind is not enough; they need insects and birds. That's one of the reasons God made some plants' corollas so beautiful and fragrant. The beautiful, fragrant corolla attracts insects—bees, for example. The bees buzz from flower to flower, get some pollen stuck to their feet, then carry that pollen to other flowers. So they carry the pollen from anther to pistil, maybe to still another pistil, then pick up some more pollen—maybe from that plantís anther . . . and so on.

Bees are the most common pollen carriers. But other insects like butterflies, moths, ants, beetles, and flies can pollinate flowers too. Even some birds, like hummingbirds, help carry pollen to the flowers they visit.

Once a plant has been pollinated, the sticky chemicals on the tip of the stigma begin to dissolve the pollen's coat. Once this coat has been dissolved, the sperm cells inside the pollen slither down a special "**pollen tube**" inside the style. Once they get to the bottom of the tube, they enter the ovary where one of the sperms gets inside the ovule and puts its information together with the ovule's information so that they can produce a baby plant.

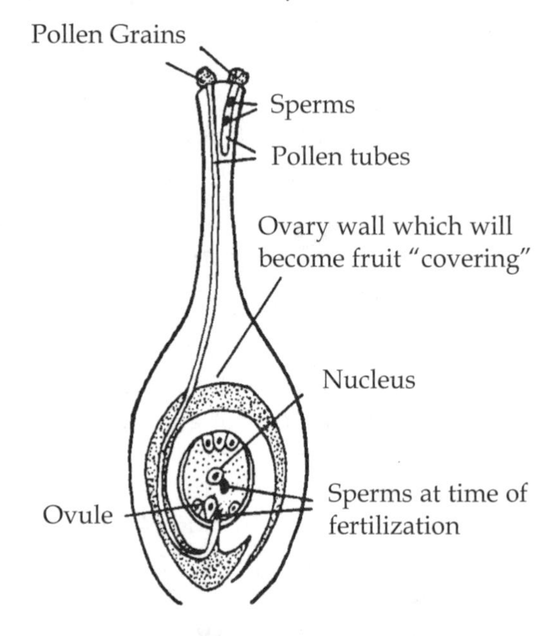

When a sperm enters an ovule, we say that the ovule has been fertilized. We call this process **fertilization**.

If they are to reproduce, most plant species require that the pollen must come from one plant and the ovule must come from another. The same flower, or flowers from the same plant, can't produce both the pollen and the ovule and have babies.

A few species, however, can produce healthy babies if the pollen and the ovule come from the same flower. Plants that are able to fertilize themselves are said to be **self-pollinating**. Species that must get their pollen from one plant and their ovules from another are called **cross-pollinators**.

Pistils are not just the place where ovules grow. They are also the place where fertilized ovules become **embryos** or baby plants—what we call **seeds**. And while embryos grow to become mature seeds, the pistils—especially the ovaries—also grow. The ovaries cover and protect the seeds inside them. If the ovary and seeds fall to the ground and the seeds begin to grow, the ovary provides food for the seed until it can grow roots and get nourishment from the soil.

You eat these enlarged ovaries all the time. When you eat them, you think of them as fruits (like apples), or pods (like green beans), vegetables (like squash or pumpkins), or nuts (like acorns and chestnuts).[4]

Laboratory Exercise

1. Find a flower and identify its parts. (A good flower to look at is a gladiolus.) Can you find the calyx with its sepals? The corolla with its petals? The pistil(s)? The stamens? If you can, look at some other flowers too.

2. Go through fruits, nuts, and vegetables that your family eats: what "nuts" are seeds? Which fruits do we tend to eat and which ones do we tend to throw away? *(Example: we eat green bean fruits – the fruit [pod] as well as the seed; but we tend only to eat the seeds of peas and throw out the mature pea ovary [the pod].)* What about apples and oranges?

3. Come up with a hypothesis why there are so many seeds in the fruit of an apple? *(Suggestion: The ovary of an apple flower has many ovules in it which all become fertilized and form seeds.)* What hypothesis would you like to suggest for why orange fruits not only have many seeds, but lots of separate segments inside? *(Suggestion: The orange flower not only has many ovules, but many ovaries that combine to form what we think of as a "single fruit".)*

---

[4]Note: Most nuts are *not* ovaries; they are seeds. The walnut, the cashew, and the Brazil nut are examples. The peanut that we eat is a seed, but it grows in a very peculiar manner. (Look it up in an encyclopedia!)

Vocabulary

flower—the reproductive part of a plant

reproduce—to have babies

sepal—an individual part of the calyx; it often looks like a small petal

calyx—the bud case that becomes the base of a flower

corolla—the most fragrant and colorful part of a flower; it is made up of petals

petal—an individual piece of the corolla

gamete—also called a sex cell or reproductive cell; it contains half of the design information necessary in order to make a baby; a male gamete and a female gamete must be put together in order to make a baby

stamen—the male reproductive organ in a plant consisting of a filament and an anther

pistil—the female reproductive organ in a plant consisting of the ovary, style and stigma

filament—the long base of the stamen

anther—the tip *of the stamen that produces pollen*

pollen—produced by the stamen; each grain of pollen contains two male gametes called sperms

sperm—the male reproductive cell or gamete

ovary—the base of the pistil which produces ovules

ovule—the female reproductive cell or gamete

style—the mid-part of the pistil that supports the stigma

stigma—the sticky tip of the pistil that catches pollen

pollination—the name for what happens when pollen becomes stuck to the stigma

pollen tube—a structure that grows down from the stigma to the ovary and through which the sperms travel in order to fertilize the ovules

fertilization—what happens when a sperm enters an ovule

self-pollinator—a plant whose sperms can fertilize its own ovules

cross-pollinator—a plant that requires sperms from another plant[5] to fertilize its ovules

embryo—baby plant

seed—what is produced when an ovule is fertilized; it contains a plant embryo and can grow into a complete new plant

Questions

- ✦ What are the three main parts of a plant? *(The roots, the stem, and the leaves.)*
- ✦ Why do plants have flowers? *(A flower is the part of the plant that makes it able to have babies.)* What do flowers make? *(seeds and fruits or pods)*
- ✦ What are the four main parts of a flower? *(The calyx, the corolla, the stamen[s] and the pistil[s].)*
- ✦ What kinds of information do cells store inside themselves? *(Operational information—so they can stay alive; and design information—so they can reproduce after their kind.)*
- ✦ Why do plants need to have *both* a mother *and* a father? *(Because the male and female [father and mother] gametes each have only half the information they need to make a new plant.)*
- ✦ Name at least two things that help pollinate flowers. *(wind, insects [like bees], and birds)*

[5]Another plant in the same species!

MONOCOTS AND DICOTS

There are two main types or classes[1] of angiosperms (covered-seed plants): **monocotyledons** (MAW-no- COT'l-ee-d'ns, or **monocots**: "single seed-leaf" plants) and **dicotyledons** (DIE-cot'l-ee-d'ns, or **dicots**: "double seed-leaf" plants).

When a seed is big enough, it isn't too hard to tell whether it is a monocot or a dicot. You can tell just by looking at it. Simply open it up and see if it tends to split in two or wants to remain a single piece. **Di-** means *two,* and **mono-** means *one.* For example, peas tend to split in two; they are dicots. But corn seeds are of one piece; corn is a monocot.

Seeds

We have said that seeds contain baby plants. They already have a tiny plant inside of them, complete with a root ready to grow and some food to give the plant energy until it is old enough to make its own food from sunlight.

Laboratory Exercise

Let's take a look at some real seeds.

What You Will Need:

- A few beans (lima beans are especially good) or peanuts and some kernels of corn. You may also want to try some other large seeds (pea, grapefruit, orange, etc.). Let any dried seeds (except peanuts) soak in water at least overnight

[1]Remember: Kingdom, Phylum, Class, Order, Family, Genus, Species. . . .

- Tweezers
- Magnifying glass (optional)

Start with a bean or a peanut. In my example I will look at a bean. You may find some minor differences if you look at another seed.

Look carefully at a bean seed. (Remember that the first step a scientist uses is observation.)

Method:

Hold your bean so that the flat edge of the bean faces you. Notice the scar, called the **hilum**, where the bean was once attached to its pod. If you are using peanuts, you need to open the "shell" first and see the "nuts" inside. (The peanut shell is actually the dried pod, or fruit, around the seeds inside.)

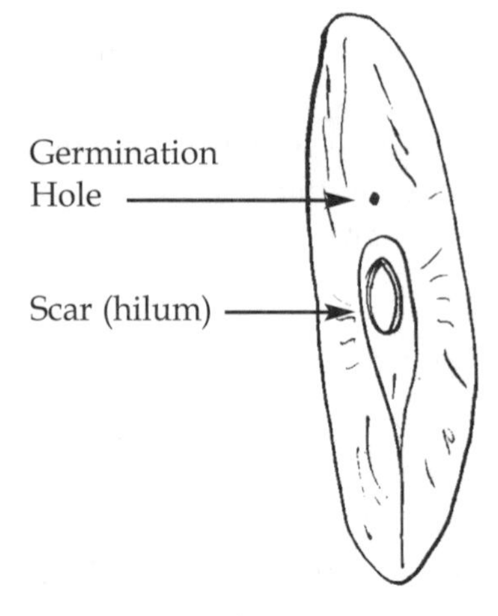

Outside of a Bean Seed

Above (or below) the hilum is a tiny hole. You may need a magnifying glass to see it. This hole, called a germination hole, is where the sperm got into the ovule (which has now become a bean seed).

Now, using your tweezers, carefully peel off the thin white bean seed coat. This should have separated from the bean while it was being soaked.

If you are using a peanut, the seed coat is the dark papery "skin" covering the "nut" (peanut "nuts" are actually seeds!). If you are extra careful, you can separate a lima bean's seed coat into two very thin layers. The **seed coat** helps protect the baby plant until it is ready to grow.

Now, take a look at the bean or peanut seed without its skin. Do you see that it has a crack across the top and running down two of its sides? At its base, there is a little thing that sticks out. That thing is the baby plant's first root!

Now, insert a fingernail or knife blade in the crack at the top of the seed and gently separate its two halves. Be very careful!

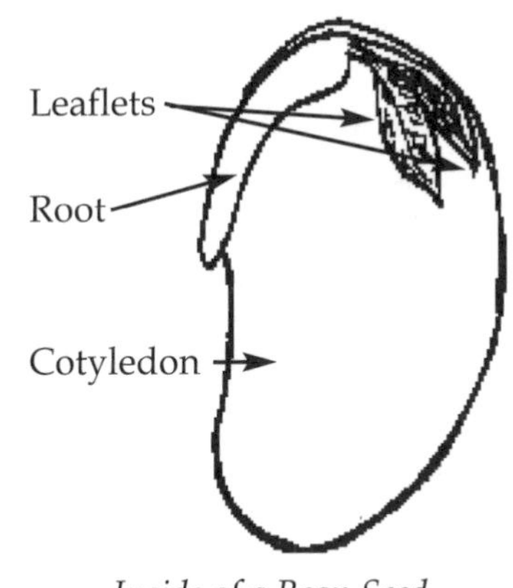

Inside of a Bean Seed

Each of these two halves is a cotyledon. In the same way that a mature plant's leaves produce food for it to eat, **cotyledons** store and release food for the baby plant to use while it is beginning to grow.

Question:

Based on what you can see, is a bean (or peanut) a monocot or a dicot? Why? *(It is a dicot because it has two ["di-" or "two"] "halves" or "seed leaves".)*

Let's continue with our investigation.

Notice that a small structure is still attached to one of the cotyledons. This is the **embryo**, the part of the seed that will become the mature plant. If you look very closely, you might be able to recognize two tiny **leaflets** and a small fingerlike bump that will become the plant's first root.

When you carefully break and cut something apart so you can see all its parts, scientists say you are **dissecting** it. Now that you have dissected a bean or peanut, you might want to try dissecting a kernel of corn. Can you locate the seed coat? The cotyledon(s)? The leaflets? The baby root?

Based on your observation of its seed, is corn a monocot or a dicot? *(a monocot)*

Further Research:

If you have extra seeds that you have soaked, you can try growing them. Put some damp cotton in a clean clear plastic or glass cup. Place the seeds between the cotton and the side of the cup so that you can see them. Arrange them so that they are in different positions. Place the cup in a warm (70°F or 21°C) place until the seed starts to grow. Then move it into bright light, such as near a window. (Note: Direct sunlight may be too strong for a baby plant.) Unfortunately, if your seeds are very old, or if they have been kept very warm, they may be dead and won't sprout.

In a few days, the root will begin to emerge from between the cotyledons. Notice that the root always grows down, no matter which direction you plant the bean.

How does this help the plant? *(The root will always grow into the soil.)*

Watch the leaflets start to grow. Which way do they grow? *(They will grow upward, towards the top of the soil and the sunlight.)*

Vocabulary

monocotyledon—a seed that has only a single store of food

dicotyledon—a seed that has two cotyledons or stores of food

hilum—scar from where a bean seed was attached to its pod

seed coat—an extremely thin protective covering or "skin"

cotyledon—"seed leaf," a store of food for the embryo

embryo—the baby plant itself that will grow into an adult plant

leaflet—immature first "true" leaf within a seed

dissect—to cut apart in order to analyze

Other Ways to Tell a Monocot from a Dicot

If scientists are looking at a plant and can't find its seeds, or if its seeds are too small, they will use four other ways of deciding if a plant is a monocot or a dicot. Each of these characteristics is almost always true of all monocots and dicots. If you find that a particular plant has at least two or three characteristics that agree, you can be sure you have made the right identification.

1. Leaves

- ✦ A dicot's leaves have veins that branch out from a single main "artery" in the center. The veins form a network.
- ✦ A monocot's leaves have parallel veins.

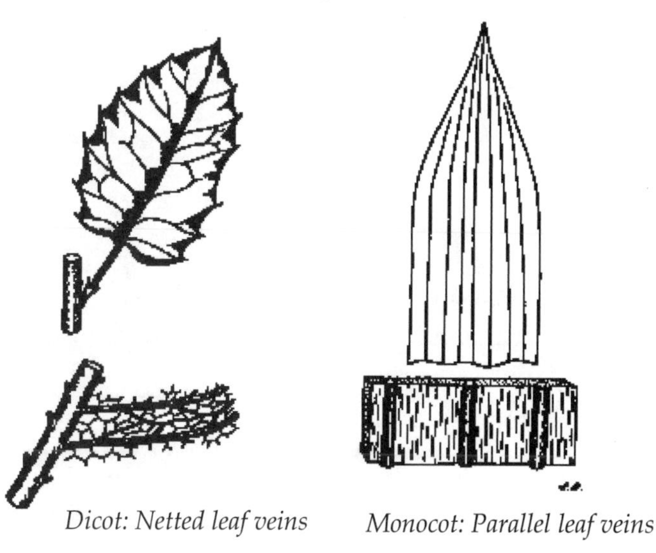

Dicot: Netted leaf veins *Monocot: Parallel leaf veins*

Laboratory Exercise

Look at a variety of leaves (e.g., a maple leaf, the leaf of an apple tree, a blade of grass, the leaf of an ear of corn). Based on their leaves, what kinds of plants are these? *(Maples and apples are dicots; grass and corn are monocots.)*

2. Veins and Vascular System

- ✦ Dicots' xylem and phloem are arranged in a ring right at the outside, or growth edge, of a stem or branch (in a tree, for instance, outside of the wood and inside of the bark).
- ✦ Monocots' vessels seem to be spread randomly throughout the stem of the plant.

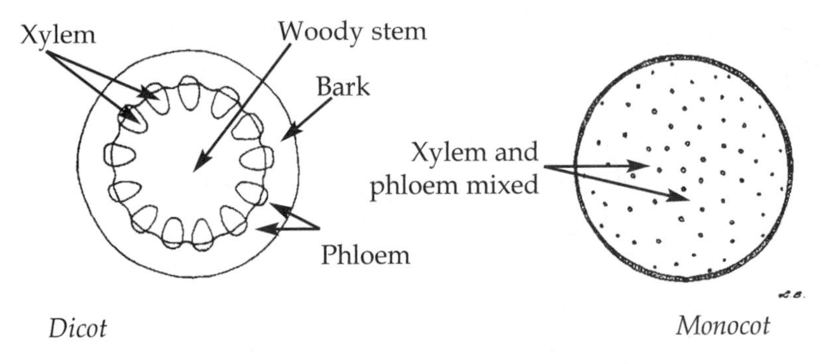

Dicot *Monocot*

Laboratory Exercise

Based on its vessels, is grass a monocot or a dicot? *(monocot)* How about a prune, plum, apple or pear tree? *(all dicots)*

3. Flower Patterns

Flower patterns aren't always as helpful as are the arrangement of vessels and the leaf pattern in determining whether a plant is a mono- or dicot, but still, in general:

- ✦ The parts of a monocotyledon's flowers almost always come in multiples of three (three, six, nine, etc.).
- ✦ Dicotyledons' flowers are usually in fives, but can be in twos or fours.

Dicot *Monocot*

Laboratory Exercise

Do you have some flowers in your garden or a book that shows good pictures of flowers? If so, see if you can identify some monocots and some dicots. To make sure you have some of both, you may want to look at a plum, a cherry, a lily, a Trillium, and a Yucca.

4. Roots

Root systems are the least accurate when it comes to telling you whether you are looking at a monocot or a dicot. Still,

- ✦ Dicotyledons usually have taproots: one strong root with a few fibers off to the sides.

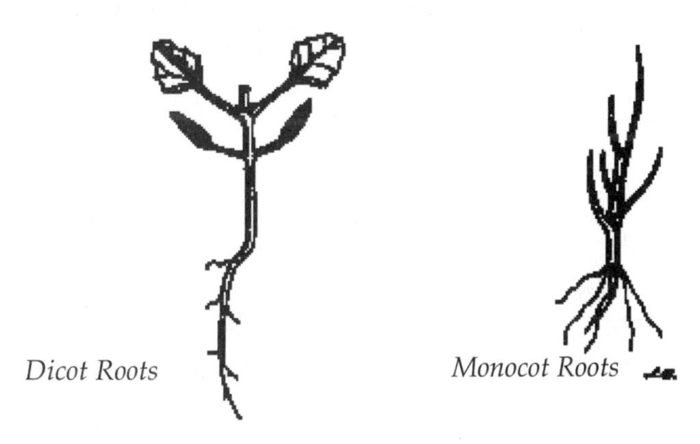

Dicot Roots *Monocot Roots*

✦ Monocotyledons have fibrous roots: All the roots are about the same size with no single root being much bigger than the others.

Laboratory Exercise

Try looking at the roots of a few weeds around your house. Compare them to the roots of your grass. Do the taproot plants have flowers that show the typical pattern for dicots, or do they break the rules? Based on your observations, are turnips and/or beets monocots or dicots? *(dicots)*

Question

1. What are the five methods you can use to help determine whether a plant is a monocot or a dicot?

   a. examine the ***seed*** *itself: does it tend to split in half (dicot) or is it a single piece (monocot);*

   b. examine the ***leaves****: netted=dicot, parallel veins=monocot;*

   c. examine the ***vascular system*** *in the stem: xylem and phloem in a ring at the edges=dicot; xylem and phloem throughout the stem=monocot;*

   d. examine ***flowers****: petals in multiples of five, four or two= dicot; multiples of three=monocot;*

   e. examine the ***roots****: tap root=dicot, fibrous roots=monocot)*

Further Activities

✦ Make a chart that summarizes the five primary methods of differentiating mono- and dicots.

✦ Use the five methods to determine whether celery is a mono- or dicot. The stem structure is a bit tricky: pay attention to what tubular structures are actually xylem and phloem. (Remember the food coloring experiment back on page 36!)

OTHER WAYS THAT SCIENTISTS DISTINGUISH BETWEEN PLANTS

Once we get down to the level of monocots and dicots, we have distinguished the biggest groups of plants. Beyond this point, the number of different groupings explodes.

Rather than naming all the different groups, we will look at some of the features that help scientists to know what kinds of plants they are looking at. Then when you look at plants, you will be able to categorize them the same way!

A. Roots

Primary and Secondary Roots

The first part of a baby plant to come out of the seed is the tip of the root. (If you sprouted bean seeds in the last section, you would have seen this.) This first root is called the **primary** (first) **root**. Very quickly, other roots branch off of the primary root. These are called **secondary roots**. As we already mentioned concerning monocots and dicots, when there is one major primary root, and all the secondary roots are tiny, the plant is said to have a **taproot** system. If the plant's roots are all about the same size, the roots are said to be **fibrous** (see monocot roots picture, pp. 57-58).

Adventitious Roots

While most roots form underground and branch off the primary root, some roots can form out of the stem or even from the leaves of a plant. These are called **adventitious** roots. Corn, sugar cane and banyan trees all form adventitious roots at the base of their stems to give additional support to the stem.

Other plants, like mistletoe, dodder and the Indian paintbrush, are called parasites. These **parasites** use adventitious roots to get food and water from other plants, called **hosts**, rather than from the soil. Their roots penetrate these host plants and pull food and water from the xylem and phloem of these plants.

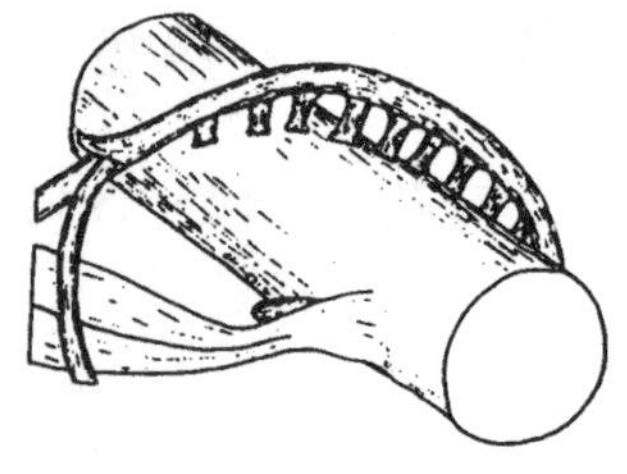

Dodder adventitious roots feeding off a wild buckwheat stem.

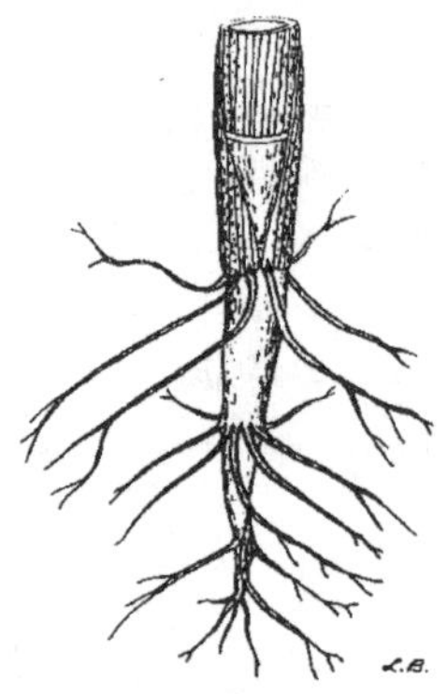

Indian corn adventitious roots provide additional support to the plant.

Gardeners can start new plants by encouraging a cut stem of a plant to produce adventitious roots. If you cut a piece of the stem off of certain plants, then put the cut end into water, the stem will produce roots—adventitious roots. Once these adventitious roots have formed, you can plant the stem in soil, and the new roots will support the plant for life.

Storage Roots

Some plants' roots become storage depots for food. Roots that store food become thicker than normal. Carrot roots (the part of the carrot we eat), beets, turnips and sweet potatoes are all forms of **storage roots**.

White potatoes and yams, though they grow underground, are not storage roots! They are something botanists call tubers. **Tubers**, though they serve much the same function as storage roots and though they usually do grow underground, are actually part of a plant's stem. They are not roots.

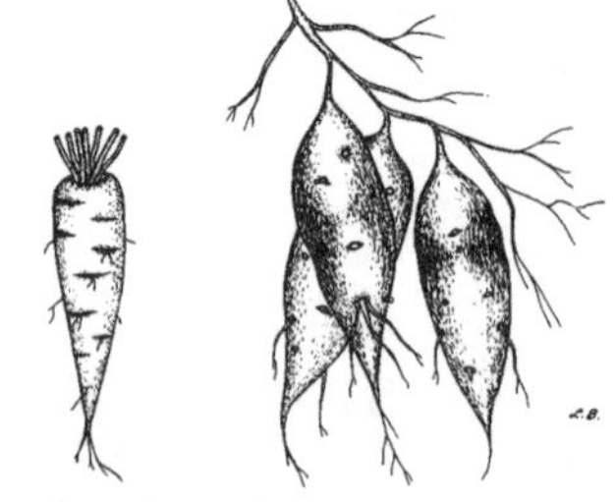

Carrot and sweep potato plants have storage roots—which are the portions of these plants that we eat.

Laboratory Exercises

1. Can you find the primary root of a carrot? How about a carrot's secondary roots?
2. What kinds of roots does the grass around your house have? *(should be fibrous)*
3. Try to produce some adventitious roots on a cutting from a house plant you like. Cut a piece off the end of one of a plant's stems. Place the cut end so the cut is under water while the major part of the stem is in the air. See if the stem will produce new roots. (Spider plants, ivies, and other non-woody plants will do very well in water. Geraniums are remarkable in that you can cut them, stick them directly in moist dirt, and they will produce roots very quickly—a week or two at most.)

Vocabulary

primary root—the first root to come directly out of the seed

secondary root—a root that branches out of the primary root

taproot—a thick primary root where only relatively tiny secondary roots grow

fibrous root—a root system where all the roots are close to the same size

adventitious root—a root that grows out of the stem

parasite—a plant that acquires its food and water from other plants

host—a plant that provides food and water to a parasite

storage root—a root that stores food for the plant

tuber—a thickened part of the stem that stores food for a plant

B. Stems

Basic Stem Types

For thousands of years, people have divided plants into three categories: herbs (ERBS), shrubs, and trees. These three categories are based solely on the form of the plants' stems.

- ✦ **Herbs** have soft stems. When frost hits, the stem (and, often, the plant itself) dies.
- ✦ **Shrubs** and trees have woody stems. Shrubs have no main trunk; instead, they have many branches coming right from the ground.
- ✦ **Trees**, unlike shrubs, have one main trunk and many branches off that trunk somewhere above the ground.

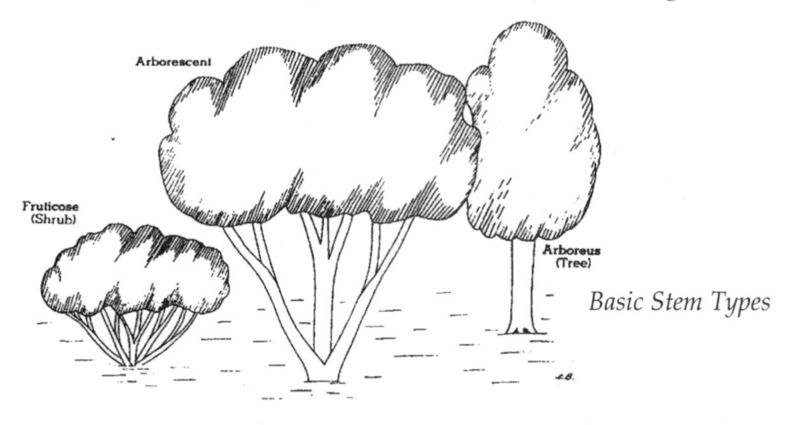

Basic Stem Types

Besides the herbs, shrubs and trees, there are many plants that come in between. "**Arborescent**" plants, for instance, are "tree-like" plants ("arbor" means tree; "-escent" means like); they have heavy, wooden limbs, but the main trunk is very short. They appear almost as if they are overgrown shrubs or trees with several trunks. Other plants are "shrub-like" (**suffruticose**). A shrub's entire stem structure survives the winter. A suffruticose plant has the same basic stem structure as a shrub, except only a few inches of stem survives above the ground year after year; the tips of the stems die. Rose bushes are often suffruticose.

Direction of Growth

Have you noticed that different plants grow in different directions? Some plants, like tulips, stand straight up. Others lie flat on the ground. Here are some of the various directions plants tend to grow, and the scientific names for them:

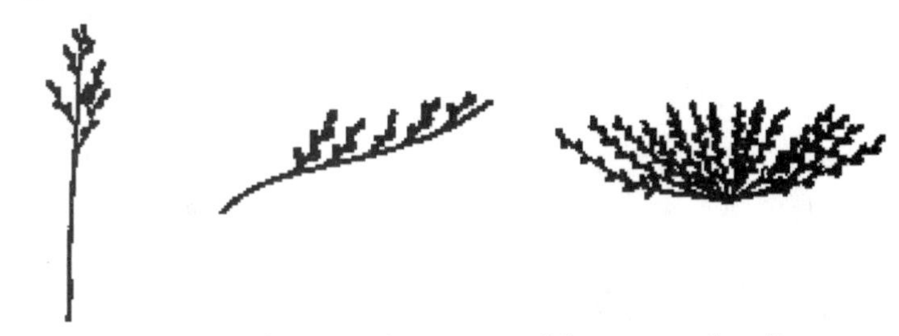

Straight up: ***erect.***

Bending over in one direction: ***declined.***

Many stems bending over in all directions: ***diffuse.***

Lying on the ground, but trying to stand up (the tip of each stem pointing upwards): ***decumbent.***

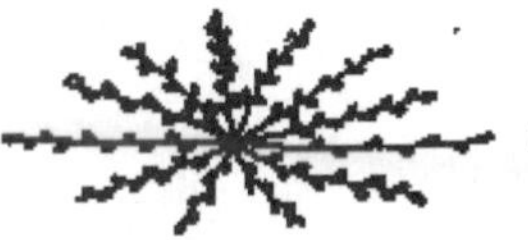

Lying flat on the ground: ***procumbent.***

Lying on the ground and producing adventitious roots: ***creeping.***

Question

- ✦ What are some of the ways scientists classify plant stems? *(by whether they are woody [trees, shrubs] or soft [herbs]; whether there is one main stem [trees] or many stems coming out of the ground [shrubs]; and then the direction of growth: erect, declined, diffuse, decumbent, precumbent, creeping or climbing)*

Vocabulary

herb—having a soft stem

shrub—having many woody stems all coming out of the ground

tree—having a single major woody stem that then branches above ground

arborescent[1]—"tree-like": having a very short above-ground stem that almost immediately branches into many stems

suffruticose—shrub-like in structure, yet dying back in the winter

Laboratory Exercise

See if you can find at least one plant that shows each of the stem growth patterns we have discussed.

Special Stem Types

Stolons

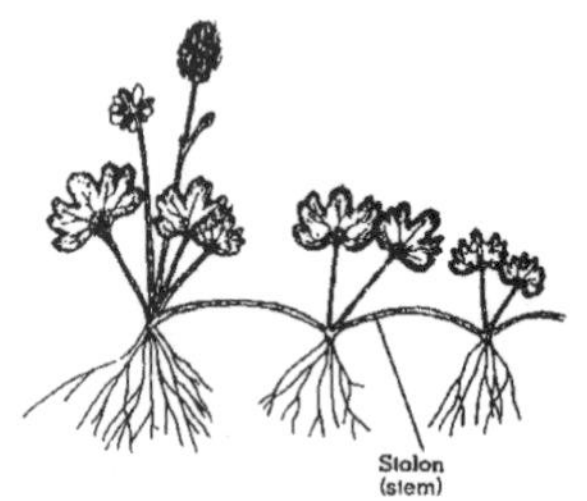

Strawberry plants put out special stems called **stolons** (pronounced like the word stolen). The stolons will grow maybe eight inches or a foot long, then develop adventitious roots and, above the roots, a strawberry plant. Suddenly, instead of just one strawberry plant, you will have two. In fact, since when a strawberry plant produces one stolon it will probably produce several, you probably won't have just two strawberry plants, you will have six or seven: the main parent plant, plus the five or six babies, each attached to the parent by its own stolon. Once a baby plant has begun, stolons will continue to grow another six or eight inches and produce another plant . . . and so forth. If you are willing to let your strawberry plants grow in this way, you can multiply them very quickly.[2]

---

[1]"Arbor" is a good word to memorize; it is used relatively frequently. The United States has an annual Arbor Day: a day dedicated to planting trees.

[2]There is only one potential problem with letting them behave like this: you won't get many strawberries! God has made all plants and animals to produce babies. Since strawberries can have babies in either of two ways—by making seeds or making stolons—they will use whichever means seems most likely to be successful. If it is kept from reproducing through stolons, then it will produce fruit. But if stolons work, then it won't "put out the effort" to produce fruit!

Rhizomes

Rhizomes are like stolons in that they are also stems and produce other plants. **Rhizomes** are different from stolons in that they grow underground while stolons grow above. Some rhizomes are skinny-like the rhizomes of Bermuda grass. Other rhizomes are fat. If you have ever grown irises, you know what I am talking about. Immediately beneath the surface of the soil, you will find huge, rootlike structures. These are rhizomes. They look like roots, but they are not roots. The iris roots come out of the bottom of the iris rhizomes.

Probably the most famous rhizome is the white potato-like the potatoes you buy in the store. Ginger is also a rhizome. However, when a rhizome thickens like a potato, that portion of the rhizome is called a **tuber**.

Laboratory Exercises

1. Visit your yard or a nearby garden. See how many different kinds of stems you can find and name. Can you find an herb? A shrub? A tree? An arborescent plant?
2. If you have a lawn, does it propagate by creeping? Does it use rhizomes?
3. Try growing a strawberry plant. Take note of the stolons.
4. Get some Bermuda grass or an iris. See if you can tell the difference between the stolon(s) and the roots.

Vocabulary

stolon—a "runner": a special stem that puts out adventitious roots and creates baby plants

rhizome—a stem that grows underground and puts out roots and creates baby plants

tuber—a fat rhizome that stores food for the plant (or for an animal that eats it!)

C. Flowers

Flowers come in many shapes and sizes. So you can get an idea of the variety of designs God has made, we will list some of the flower shapes botanists have noticed.

Let's start with the most obvious forms.

Symmetry

One of the simplest things to see in a flower is its **symmetry** (side-to-side equality of size and shape). Some flowers can be divided across their centers in virtually any direction, and both sides will look like mirror images of each other. These are called radially symmetrical (they "have **radial symmetry**"). Other flowers are equal side-to-side only if you split them in one direction. A flower that is symmetrical in only one direction is said to be **bilaterally symmetrical**.

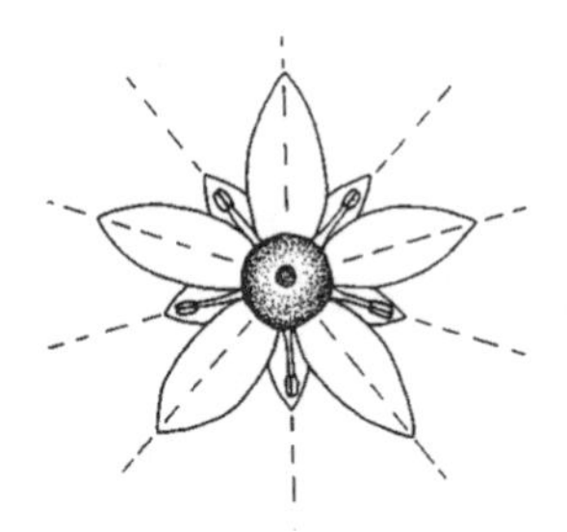

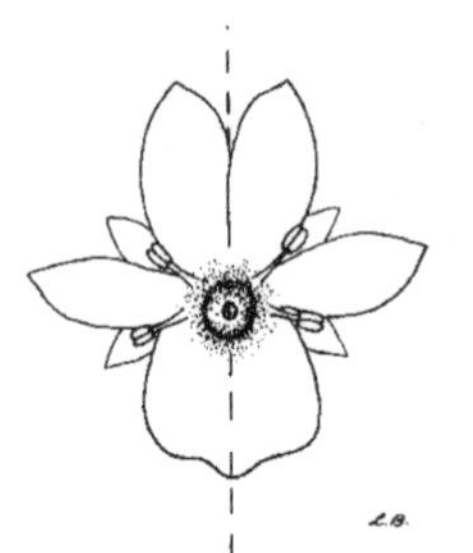

A ***radially symmetrical*** *flower*

A ***bilaterally symmetrical*** *flower*

Corollas

Have you ever noticed that flower petals come in different shapes and sizes? Most flowers' petals are all separate (**choripetalous**), but some are only partly separate (**sympetalous**), and some flowers don't have any petals at all (**apetalous**)!

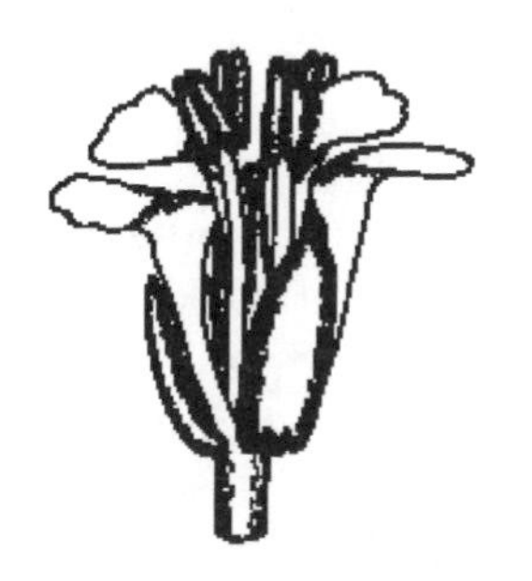

The ***choripetalous*** *flower of a mustard*

The ***sympetalous*** *flower of a bindweed or morning glory*

The ***apetalous*** *flower of the goosefoot*

Calyxes (Bud Covers)

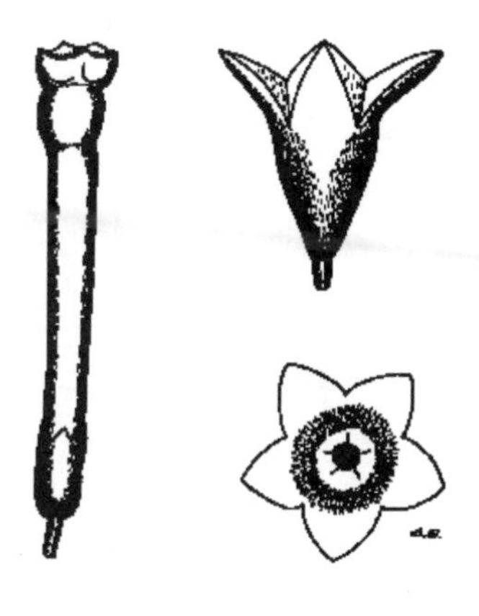

Calyxes, just like corollas, are sometimes made of individual sepals and sometimes of sepals that are joined together. And just as corollas come in different shapes and sizes, so, too, do calyxes. Here are pictures of flowers that have tubular calyxes. On the left is a tree tobacco flower. It has a tubular calyx and a tubular corolla. On the right are side and top views of the Sterculia flower, which has a calyx—a tubular calyx—but no corolla! The calyx is the main part of the flower that you will see.

Stamens and Pistils

The flowers of different species of plant normally have different numbers of stamens and pistils. Some plants' flowers have just a few stamens; others have dozens. Some flowers have just one single, solitary pistil. Others have many pistils.

Composite Flowers

Some of the things we think of as single flowers are really many, many flowers bunched up together. These are called **composite flowers**. Botanists have identified about 20,000 different species of plants that grow composite flowers. You are probably familiar with daisies, sunflowers, and dandelions. What we think of as a single daisy or sunflower is really dozens of tiny flowers. In the center are hundreds of **disk florets**. Around the outside, what look like petals are really **ray florets**. If you were to pull one of these composite flowers apart, you would find that each disk floret is really a complete flower, and each ray floret is a complete flower as well.

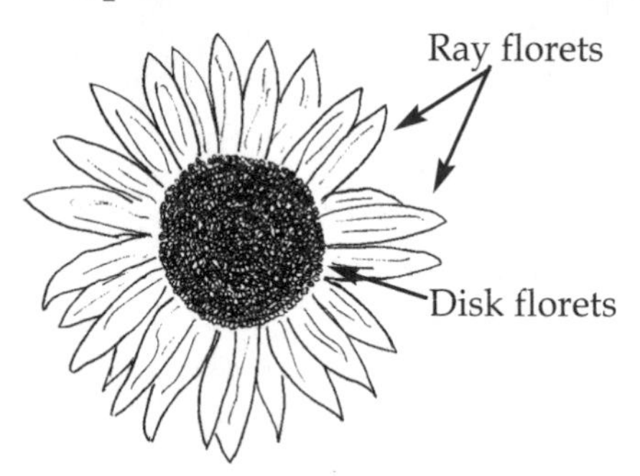

Typical Composite Flower

Vocabulary

symmetry – side-to-side equality of size and shape

radial symmetry – symmetry if you look at it from any of many different directions

bilateral symmetry – symmetry if you look at it in only one particular way

choripetalous – having separate petals

sympetalous – having petals that are only partially separate from each other

apetalous – having no petals ("a-" is a prefix that means "no")

composite flowers – something that looks like a single flower, but is actually made up of many, many tiny flowers (called "florets") that are of two distinct types: "ray" and "disk" florets

disk florets—the tiny flowers in a composite flower that look like the center area—where the stamen(s) and pistil(s) are—in a normal flower; all together, the disk florets make a round, disk shape

ray florets—the tiny flowers in a composite flower that make up what looks like the composite flower's ***corolla*** or petals

Laboratory Exercises

1. Collect some flowers and see how many different arrangements and varieties of calyxes, corollas, pistils and stamens you can find. Be sure to include some composite flowers.
2. Have you found any plants where the stamens, the calyx, or the pistil(s) are more colorful or noticeable than the petals? (Try looking at dogwood or poinsettias; the red flowers of the bottlebrush shrubs and trees are most noticeable for their stamens.)

Conclusion

We could go on describing differences botanists have found among flowers and plants, but it would take forever. Perhaps you will want to become a botanist and study these matters when you get to college!

We have looked at the differences in plants as seen in their seeds, roots, stems and flowers. Perhaps you could do a little study to consider how they differ in their leaves?

Laboratory Exercise

See how many different kinds of leaves you can find. Look for leaves that are: scaly, needle-like, broad and flat, thick and round, jagged-edged, smooth-edged, composite (a single leaf, but appearing as if it is many leaves). How about a web-veined leaf versus a parallel-veined leaf (remember one of the differences between monocots and dicots)? A hairy-surfaced leaf and a smooth-surfaced leaf? What other kinds of leaves can you find?

Questions for Further Study

1. What does a cactus leaf look like? (Hint: Cactus leaves don't look like leaves at all!) *(Cactus leaves are the spines!)*
2. So what do cactus stems look like? *(That's right: those big chunky things are actually cactus stems!)*
3. Perhaps you can do a little research to find out why botanists think God designed cacti as He did. What advantages do they gain from their unusual structures?
4. Are the fleshy parts of cacti the above-ground equivalents of *tubers*? Why or why not?

THE ANIMAL KINGDOM

Biologists say there are well over one million (maybe even two million!) or more species of animals. But that doesn't necessarily mean there are one- or two-million different "kinds" of animals like God meant in Genesis 1, or even in the sense that people two hundred years ago used the word.

But scientists today have found more than a million animals that are different enough from one another that they figure they must be of different groups.

Just like botanists who categorize plants, zoologists look at certain physical characteristics to decide whether an animal belongs to one category or another.[1] Then, once they have decided the category, they organize the categories according to how complex the animals in each group are.

There are several phyla (or phylums) of animals. One of the main phyla is those with nerve cords (called *chordates*—CORE-dates). Most of the animals with nerve cords are called vertebrates (VER-tih-brehts or VER-teh-brates) because they have bones in their backs called vertebrae (VER-teh-bray). The vertebrae surround and protect the nerve cord. (In our own bodies, we call the nerve cord and the vertebrae that surround it our spinal column.)

So whenever they find a new animal, the first question zoologists ask is: "Does the animal have a backbone?" If the answer is yes, then the animal is a vertebrate; if the answer is no, then it is an invertebrate. We will start our study with the vertebrates.

---

[1]They also consider embryonic development, biochemistry, and genetic information.

Phylum[2]*: Vertebrates*

All vertebrates have a spinal nerve cord at some time in their lives.[3] Zoologists list five main types, or classes—of vertebrates: mammals, reptiles, amphibians, birds, and fishes.

Class: Mammals

When someone asks us to think of an animal, the first one we are likely to think of is usually a mammal. Dogs, cats, horses, pigs, goats, cows, raccoons: they are all mammals.

The word "mammal" comes from a Latin word, *mamma,* which means "breast." Mammals are animals that have mammary glands—glands that produce milk to feed their young.

Besides producing milk, mammals share several other features.

Mammals are the only animals that have sweat glands. Sweat glands help maintain your body temperature by cooling you off when you are hot. The perspiration, or sweat, cools you down as it evaporates. Only mammals perspire.

Mammals never have more than two pairs of limbs (four altogether).

All mammals have hair at some time in their lives, and most have an outer hair (or fur) covering. (A few are practically hairless: for instance, the whale and the elephant.)

All mammals are warm-blooded, which means they use food energy to maintain a certain temperature in their bodies. Do you know what the normal temperature of human beings is? *(about 98 or 99 degrees Fahrenheit or 37 degrees Centigrade)*

Mammals care for their young. Unlike most other animals, mammal babies cannot care for themselves when they are first born. The mother must care for them.

---

[2]Technically, "vertebrate" is a sub-phylum of the phylum "chordate" (having a nerve cord). But invertebrate chordates are simply classed among the invertebrates (animals that have no backbone).

[3]Almost all animals that have a nerve cord also have vertebrae. There are a few animals, however, that have the nerve cord, but no protective bones around it. We will deal with them later, when we cover the invertebrates.

Most mammals have teeth, and those that have teeth usually have two or three different types of teeth. You can see what I mean by looking in your own mouth. People have three types of teeth: incisors (the front teeth) for cutting, canines (the pointed teeth next to your incisors) for ripping, and molars (the broad, flat teeth in back) for grinding and chewing.

Among mammals that have teeth, they get (at most) only two sets of teeth over the course of their lives. Human beings have baby teeth, and then adult teeth when they fall out.

Animals that aren't mammals either have no teeth or may have an almost unlimited supply of teeth. Take the shark, for example. If a shark's tooth is knocked out or yanked out, another tooth will soon grow to replace it. No matter how many times you knock its teeth out, it will grow new ones.

All mammals reproduce sexually—pretty much the same way that spermatophyte plants reproduce. The father's sperm (or seed) cell unites with the mother's ovum (or egg) cell to form an embryo (or baby).

The Different Orders (Types) of Mammals

Depending on which zoologists you talk to, there are either eighteen or nineteen orders[4] of mammals. Sixteen or seventeen of those orders—all but about 260 of the thousands of mammal species in the world—are placental mammals. Placental mammals grow inside their mothers until they are ready to be born.

Placental mammal mothers have a special organ called a placenta that takes nourishment from the mothers' blood and gives it to the baby.

This is the way you were born. While you were inside your mother, your umbilicus (um-bill-I-cus) or "belly button" was attached to an umbilical cord, and the umbilical cord was attached to your mother's placenta. The placenta, then, was attached to the inside of your mother's womb, which is the place God made for babies to grow.

---

[4]Remember: *kingdom, phylum, class, order, family, genus, species.*

After they are born, placental mammals stay close to their mothers and their mothers watch over and care for them. When the babies need something to eat, they come to their mothers and get the milk they need.

The other two orders of mammals develop differently from the placentals. In fact, they develop in two different ways, and they are sorted according to the way that they develop. These other two orders, because they do not have placentas, are called non-placental mammals.

Zoologists think these two groups of mammals are less complex than the placentals and so they always talk about them first.

Order: Monotremes

The first group of non-placental mammals is called the monotremes. The duckbilled platypus and the echidnas (ee-KIGHD-nuhs) are monotremes. They lay eggs and the babies hatch out of the eggs.

Being hatched from an egg is called an oviparous (oh-VIH-per-us) method of reproduction.[5] Birds are oviparous animals.

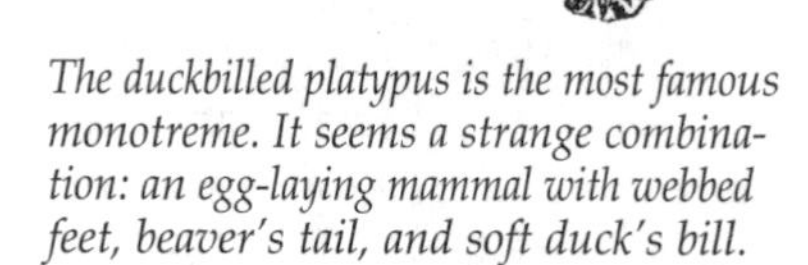

The duckbilled platypus is the most famous monotreme. It seems a strange combination: an egg-laying mammal with webbed feet, beaver's tail, and soft duck's bill.

Besides being oviparous, there are two other differences between monotremes and the other orders of mammals:

- Monotremes don't have nipples.

The echidna, or spiny anteater, lays eggs, hatches them, then carries its babies in a pouch. Its favorite food is ants and termites.

Nipples are small protruding parts of the body that have special ducts (like tiny pipes) in them that carry milk from a mother's

---

[5]Do you see the root word *ovum*, meaning *egg*, in the word oviparous?

mammary glands to the surface of her skin so her baby can get the milk it needs.

God designed monotreme mothers differently. Instead of milk ducts and nipples, He gave monotremes milk pores. Milk pores are kind of like the pores you have on your skin that let sweat come out. When a baby monotreme needs milk, instead of having to suck on its mother's nipple, it merely has to lick or "lap" milk from its mother's milk pores!

The other difference between monotremes and other mammals is that monotremes only have teeth when they are babies. When they are adults, their mouths are more like birds' beaks!

Order: Marsupials

The second order of non-placental mammals is called the marsupials (mar-SOO-pee-uhls). Kangaroos, opposums, koalas, and about 250 other animals are all marsupials.

Marsupial babies begin inside their mothers' bodies, but are born before they are strong enough to live apart from their mothers. When they are born, they crawl up their mothers' bellies to their mothers' nipples. They then attach themselves to one of their mothers' nipples and hang on there until they are big enough to get along on their own.

With its powerful hind legs and tail, the kangaroo, the most famous marsupial, can travel at 25 mph.

A koala baby is barely an inch long and about as fat as a normal lead pencil when it is born. It won't reach maturity until it is four years old.

Though marsupial babies are strong enough to hang on to their mothers' nipples, they are not strong enough to suck any milk. To make up for their babies' weakness, God has given marsupial mothers a special set of muscles next to their mammary glands that actually pump milk out of the glands, through the nipples and into the babies' mouths.

The name "marsupial" comes from a Latin word meaning pouch. Most marsupials have pouches in which their babies can ride, but a few don't, so scientists determine which animals are marsupials and which are not based on the way the babies develop rather than on whether the mothers have pouches.

Thylacine, the marsupial wolf or marsupial tiger, is the largest meat-eating marsupial. It likes to eat sheep, poultry, and wallabies.

The Tasmanian devil looks a lot like a bear cub, except for its long tail. It is not an evil creature. It got its name because of its deep, dark black color. The Tasmanian devil is almost extinct.

Except for the American opossum, all the marsupials in the world live in Australia and the islands of the South Pacific. In fact, only a few of the mammals that come from that part of the world are not marsupials! That part of the world has marsupials that look like rabbits, moles, cats, wolves . . . and even tigers!

After the monotremes and the marsupials, all the remaining mammals are placentals.

When baby opossums are born, they are barely as large as bumble bees. The tiny babies have to scramble up their mothers bellies as quickly as possible to find a nipple because, thought a litter of 'possums may include twenty babies, the mother has only thirteen nipples at most. All the "extra" babies will die. 'Possums are the only marsupials that come from North America.

Vocabulary

vertebrate – having a backbone that surrounds the spinal chord

invertebrate – having no backbone

mammal – the class of animals that has mammary glands; they are also warm-blooded, sweat, have teeth, have no more than two pairs of limbs (i.e., four limbs, total) . . .

mammary gland – a special gland that produces milk

warm-blooded – uses food energy to maintain a certain body temperature

incisor – chisel-shaped tooth used for cutting

canine – pointed tooth used for ripping

molar – relatively flat-topped tooth used for grinding

nipple – small protruding part of the body that has special ducts to carry milk from a mother's mammary glands to the surface of her skin

duct – a tiny pipe-like structure

pore – a small hole that permits liquid to go through

placenta – a special organ that takes nourishment from the mothers' blood and gives it to her baby

placental – having a placenta

non-placental – not having a placenta

monotreme – an oviparous mammal that has milk ducts rather than nipples and a beak-like mouth when it is an adult

oviparous – hatching from an egg

marsupial – a mammal whose young are born so weak and tiny that they can't suck milk; their mothers actually pump milk into their babies' mouths. Many marsupials have pouches in which they carry their young

Question

1. Name at least five distinguishing features of mammals.

   a. *they have mammary glands;*

b. *they are warm-blooded;*

c. *they sweat;*

d. *they have hair;*

e. *they have teeth;*

f. *they have no more than two pairs of limbs;*

g. *they never have more than two sets of teeth;*

h. *they have different types of teeth;*

i. *they bear their young before the young can care for themselves, so the mothers care for their young;*

j. *they reproduce sexually*

Order: Insectivores

There are about 380 species of insectivores. The name insectivore means insect-eater. Just because they are called insectivores does not mean that insectivores all eat insects; nor does it mean that other mammals don't eat insects. But insectivores have many, extremely small, sharp teeth that are well-designed for crushing insects. They also have long snouts, flat feet, and five-toed claws that are very useful for digging.

The four-inch long American short-tailed shrew helps farmers by killing insects and rodents. It has a poison very similar to the cobra's.

The insectivores most Americans are familiar with are the moles and hedgehogs.

Order: Dermopteras (der-MOP-ter-uhs)

By looking at the name, can you figure out what dermopteras do? Dermo comes from the Latin word for "skin," and Ptera means "wing," from the same Latin word that "pteridophytes" (ferns), "pterodactyl" and "archaeopteryx" come from.

The dermopteras are "skin-winged" animals—the "flying lemurs."

Dermopteras have skin flaps between their back and front legs that they use like sailplane wings. They jump off tall trees and use their skin flaps to glide to other trees. When the air is still, they can glide for seventy yards or more! Zoologists say there are only two species of dermopteras and both of them live in Southeast Asia—between the Philippines and Thailand.

The flying lemur can glide with ease, but if it ever finds itself on the ground, it is practically helpless. It sleeps during the day, hanging from a branch by its four feet.

Order: Chiropteras (ky-ROP-ter-uhs)

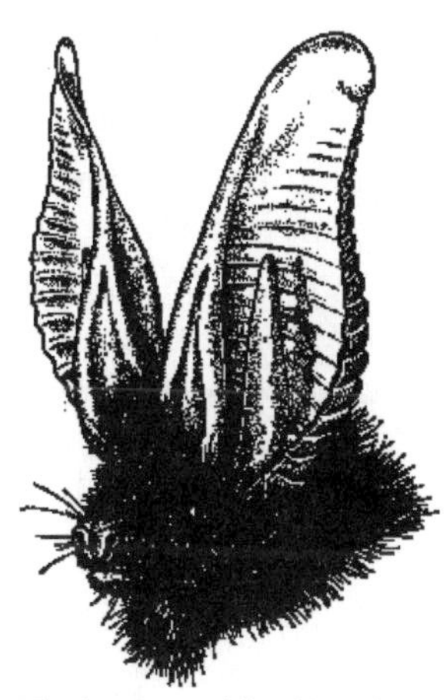

The long-eared bat lives in Europe and Africa. Its ears are almost as big as its body. It uses its ears to locate the insects it likes to eat.

"Chiro" comes from the Greek word for "hand." Can you figure out what chiropteras are? That's right: they are "hand wing" creatures. We know them as bats. There are about 900 different species of chiropteras.

Chiropteras, or bats, come in all shapes and sizes. The largest chiroptera, the "flying fox," has a five-foot wingspan. The smallest one is no larger than a hummingbird. Some bats have long tails, like mice; some have no tails. Some have tiny ears; others have huge ears that fold up like accordions. Some have feet with suction cups on the end (for sticking to smooth surfaces); others have claws.

The reason zoologists class all bats together as one order is because they all have "arm wings." If you look at a bat closely, you can see how God made the bones that we expect to be their front legs to be longer and lighter weight. Also, in between those bones, God stretched large, thin, skin wings.

Bats' wings extend from the equivalent of their pointer fingers all the way back to their hind legs and, in many bats, over their tails. Bats don't merely glide, the way the dermopteras do; they use their wings to fly—just like birds.

The hoary bat of North America has a wingspread of fifteen inches. Despite its size, it likes to eat insects. Here it is shown in the act of catching a Luna moth for dinner.

Bats live everywhere in the world except near the north and the south poles where the temperature never gets above freezing.

Most bats eat fruit and insects, though a few eat fish, some eat meat, some draw nectar from flowers, and the vampire bat sucks blood from birds and other animals.

All bats drink water, but instead of lapping it up, like dogs or cats, they sip it in mid-flight, while skimming the surface of a lake or pond.

The flying fox has a wingspan up to five feet across. Its body can be twelve inches long. Despite its tremendous size, it eats fruit, not animals.

The vampire bat lives in the tropics – from Mexico to Brazil. It feeds on the blood of warm-blooded animals. It doesn't drink enough blood to kill on account of lost blood, but it can pass infections, including rabies.

The Mexican long-nosed bat uses its tongue to dip into the flower of the night-blooming cactus to eat the nectar that is there.

Order: Primates

Primate means "first" or "foremost." Primates are "first" among animals in only one area: certain parts of their brains are more developed than in any other creatures. In virtually every other way – in terms of sight, hearing, smell, strength, and every other physical characteristic – many other animals surpass the primates.

Primates include all the monkeys and apes. Because most zoologists think that people came from these animals, they say human beings are primates as well.[6]

---

[6]As ably demonstrated by Mark Cosgrove in his wonderful out-of-print book *The Amazing Body Human* (Grand Rapids, MI: Baker Book House, 1987), there are far more *differences* between humans and the "other" primates than there are similarities. Indeed, the differences between humans and the "other" primates are so pronounced (and the similarities so weak, while the similarities among the "other" primates are so strong) that, rather than serving as a guide to research and data collection, the evolutionary hypothesis has become "an obstruction to a meaningful analysis of data" (*op. cit.*, 16).

Cosgrove summarizes: there is not even a close approximation anywhere in the animal kingdom to "the human facial muscles, nose, out-turned lips, earlobes, chin, throat, naked skin, sweat-gland system, thermoregulatory capabilities, . . . the long maturation span, the speech center and hemispheric specializations within the brain, the human heel and arch, locking knees, curved spine, redesigned pelvis, buttock muscles, fully opposable thumbs, . . . and more. For not one of these human features do we find any sufficient connecting links to the animal world" (Ibid., 194).

Convinced as I am that human beings are *not* related to the apes nor to monkeys, you should understand that all future comments about primates refer *only* to apes and monkeys and *not* to human beings.

The South American howler monkey has an enlarged voice box that gives it an incredibly loud roar. Notice the howler's grasping tail and the "thumb" on the "foot."

But there are several reasons for the differences between primates and humans. Only human feet have arches; only in human feet are the small toes parallel to and attached to the big toe by a ligament. Primates' pelvises are shaped differently from humans'. Humans' pelvises are designed for upright walking; primates' are designed for movement on all fours. Primates lack the strength to pull themselves upright. Primates' "arms" are much longer, in proportion to their legs, than are humans'. Our arms are only about four-fifths as long as our legs; macaque monkeys' arms are about an eighth longer than their legs; the gibbon's and orangutan's arms are more than one and a half times as long as their legs; gorillas' and chimpanzees' arms are more than a third longer than their legs. And we've only begun the list of differences![7]

Most primates live in trees. They also live very close to the equator (where it is warm). Most primates have five fingers on each hand and five "toes" on each "foot."[8] Primates don't have big toes the way we do, instead, both their "feet" and hands include thumbs that are set apart from the other fingers (or "toes"). Though primates use their thumbs for holding on to

---

[7]Ibid., 126-133.

[8]You may wonder why I put quotation marks around *toes* and *foot*. As Cosgrove points out, primates really don't have true feet. Their lower limbs may best be described as a second set of arms and hands.

things, their thumbs are nowhere near as helpful to them as our thumbs are to us.

Primates can swing their arms freely both forward and backward and tend to walk around on all fours. Lemurs, monkeys and apes have relatively large eyes that are set in the front of their heads so they can look forward with ease. Some have color vision (unlike other animals). Primates' sense of smell, however, is less well-developed than other animals.

The snub-nosed langur, an Old World monkey, eats leaves. It has a protruding nose and lacks the prehensile tail of the New World monkeys. Note its "thumbs" on hands and "feet."

New World monkeys (i.e., monkeys from the Americas) have special prehensile (grasping) tails—tails that can be used to hold on to tree limbs. The New World monkeys tend to be smaller than their Old World (European, African, and Asian) cousins. They also have flat noses with nostrils that are fairly wide-spaced.

The arms of Old World monkeys are very much closer in length to their legs than are the arms of any other primates. (The arms of other primates are almost all significantly longer than their legs. See footnote below.) When Old World monkeys walk, they put their hands palm-down, flat on the ground, while the heels of their "feet" are always raised.

There are two types of Old World monkeys. One group has cheek pouches for storing food. These monkeys eat all kinds of things—from fruits and

The proboscis monkey, as its name implies, has a large nose. ("Proboscis" means nose.) Its nose can be as much as three inches long and hang below its chin!

vegetables to insects, crabs, and small birds. The second group prefers to eat leaves. Since leaves are difficult to digest, they have a more complicated digestive system than their cousins that do not eat leaves.

The orangutan can weigh up to two hundred pounds, but its home is in the trees. It builds a nest in the boughs.

Great apes—gorillas, chimpanzees, orangutans, long-armed gibbons, and siamangs—are different from monkeys in several ways. They have no tails; their arms are proportionally much longer than monkeys' arms; and their arms and shoulders are much more developed than are their legs.

When they walk on all fours, the apes support the weight of their upper bodies on the knuckles of their hands rather than on their palms. When they lope on their haunches, their ankles and the sides of their feet touch the ground (rather than the heel and the ball of the foot as in human beings).

The great apes also differ from monkeys in the way they "keep house." Monkeys don't build homes; the great apes do. They build nests. Some nests are rough platforms high up in trees, but others have roofs to protect their occupants' from the weather.

There are about 180 species of primates in the world.

The gorilla is the largest great ape and can weigh up to five hundred pounds. Notice this gorilla is sitting in the middle of his nest!

Vocabulary

prehensile—grasping, able to cling to a branch

Questions

1. What are some of the differences between human beings and primates? *(Human thumbs are fully opposable to their hands; primates' "thumbs" are not fully opposable; human feet have arches and the small toes are parallel to and attached to the big toe by a ligament; primates' toes are neither parallel to nor attached to the "thumb"; humans' pelvises are designed for upright walking; primates' are designed for movement on all fours; primates don't have the strength to pull themselves up; primates' "arms" are much longer, in proportion to their legs, than are humans'.)*

2. How can you tell the difference between a New World monkey and an Old World monkey? *(New World monkeys have prehensile tails, flat noses and widely spaced nostrils, and are smaller than their Old World counterparts; their arms also tend to be proportionally longer than the Old World monkeys' arms; Old World monkeys have protruding noses, non-prehensile tails, arms that are very much closer in length to their legs' length, and they tend to walk with palms down and "heels" off the ground.)*

3. What distinguishes the two types of Old World monkeys? *(some eat leaves, others don't)*

4. Based on its appearance, is the proboscis monkey an Old World monkey or a New World monkey? *(Old World; New World monkeys have flat noses.)*

5. What are some of the differences between apes and monkeys? *(Great apes have no tails; their arms are proportionally much longer than monkeys' arms; their arms*

Even though chimpanzees are much smaller than orangutans and gorillas, they are still considered great apes. They are certainly the most teachable of the primates. In the circus, chimps have been taught to ride bicycles, dress and undress themselves, and do carpentry!

and shoulders are much more developed than are their legs; when they walk on all fours, they support their upper bodies on the knuckles of their hands rather than on their palms; they build nests.)

Order: Edentates

The word edentate means "having no teeth." In reality, however, of all the animals in this group, only the anteaters, have no teeth. The others have teeth, but their teeth are very weak. Their teeth have only a little enamel (the hard outer coating on the outside of our teeth), and no roots (which means they can be knocked out of their mouths pretty easily). None of the edentates have incisor or canine teeth (the cutting and tearing teeth that most mammals have in the front of their mouths).

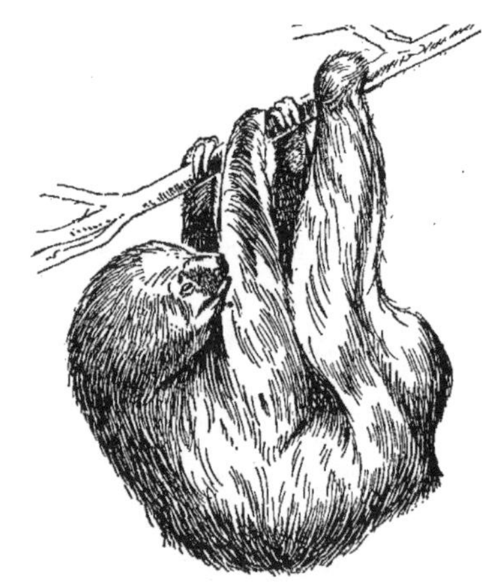

Though they lack the skin wings of the flying lemurs, tree sloths, members of the edentate family, spend their time in much the same way as flying lemurs. They hang upside down in trees. They are about as helpless on the ground as flying lemurs are, too.

Edentates are different from other mammals in another way, too. They do not keep their body temperature as stable as most mammals. When the temperature around them changes, their body temperature changes as well.

From the end of its snout to the tip of its tail, the great anteater may measure up to eight feet long! As with so many other large animals, the great anteater eats tiny pieces of food: in his case, ants!

We can divide edentates into two groups: those with hair and those with shells. Among the hairy edentates, the most common are the anteaters—which have no teeth and little mouths, but strong claws (good for tearing down anthills and termite nests) and long, extendible tongues to lap up the ants and termites when they scurry out of their destroyed homes.

Another hairy edentate is the sloth—an animal that moves extremely slowly (no more than half a mile per hour), that spends almost its entire life hanging upside down in a tree, and sleeps eighteen hours a day.

The armadillo (of which there are several types) is the most common edentate. God has given it a tough shell as special protective armor.

There are about 30 species of edentates.

The three-banded armadillo can be easily recognized by its three bands. When attacked, the armadillo curls itself into a ball. Smart dogs, however, will roll the armadillo ball into a lake. The armadillo then has to uncurl itself to catch its breath.

The nine-banded armadillo is the only edentate you're likely to see in North America. He can't see well, but if he hears you, he will run away rather quickly!

Order: Pangolins (pan-GO-luns)

Pangolins, as someone has said, look like giant pine cones. That's because, instead of hair, they have an amazing scale coat. A common name for pangolins is "scaly anteaters." If it weren't for their scaly coats, they would look exactly like other anteaters.

The common ground pangolin of Africa protects itself in the same way the armadillo does: it rolls itself up in a ball. Unlike the armadillo, however, the pangolin does not lie still. It can cause its enemy a severe injury by a swift flick of its tail.

One other difference between pangolins and other anteaters is that pangolins prefer to eat ant eggs instead of the ants themselves. Their favorites are red ant eggs.

Pangolins' scales are so hard and their coats put together so well that a man who shot a pangolin with a rifle from a hundred yards away couldn't kill it!

There are seven species of pangolins in the world and they live in Asia, Indonesia, and Africa.

Order: Aardvark

The aardvark was named by Dutch settlers who came to South Africa. Its name means "earth pig." That's because the aardvark looked to them like a pig but digs a hole in the ground and lives in it.

The aardvark is another one of those animals that looks like he was built by a committee. With his donkey ears, anteater snout, four toes in front and five in the rear, and having an overgrown, rat-like body, he is one of the world's great diggers.

Aardvarks live in Africa, weigh close to a hundred pounds, are four feet long, and have thick, heavy tails that are close to two feet long. They eat ants and termites by the millions.

There is only one species of aardvark.

Order: Lagomorphs (LAG-oh-morfs)

Lagos is the Greek word for hare and morph means "form." So the lagomorphs are the hare-like animals—hares, rabbits, and pikas.

One of the things that sets lagomorphs off from other animals is that they have two pairs of upper incisor teeth—one pair behind the other!

Hares and rabbits have large back feet and legs which they use to hop around. They also have small tails and big ears. Pikas are smaller than rabbits and hares, have shorter ears, and have front and back legs that are about the same length.

The cottontail or briar rabbit is the most common of all American rabbits.

Few people know there is a difference between hares and rabbits. In fact, in the United States, people don't bother to call hares "hares." Hares and rabbits are both called "rabbits."

The pika looks like a tiny, short-eared rabbit without a tail. It lives in rocky places and is famous for its peculiar bleating sound.

But scientists have noticed that there are differences between these animals. The biggest difference between rabbits and hares is in the way they are born. Rabbit babies are born naked (with no fur) and are unable to open their eyes at birth. Hare babies have fur and can see very well right from birth.

There are about 65 species of lagomorphs.

Order: Rodents

There are close to 1,750 species of rodents: more than all the other mammals combined!

Rodents are animals that gnaw. They have chisel-like incisor teeth at the front of both their upper and lower jaws. And whether rodents gnaw because their incisors grow or God made their incisors to grow because they gnaw, we don't know. But rodents' incisors normally never stop growing.

If one of a rodent's incisors is damaged so that it stops growing, the animal will either die of starvation (because it can't use its teeth properly), or (because it can't gnaw correctly anymore) the tooth on the opposite jaw will grow right through the space where the tooth that stopped growing used to be.

Rodents include rats, mice, beavers, squirrels, woodchucks, marmots, prairie dogs, chipmunks, gophers, muskrats, hamsters, lemmings, porcupines, and hundreds of others. They are generally broken down into three suborders: the squirrel-like rodents, the mouse-like rodents, and the "others"—the porcupines, guinea pigs, and other curiosities.

The beaver (above) is the perfect example of a rodent: a gnawer above all gnawers. It uses its teeth to cut down trees. It uses the cut wood to build its house.

If a beaver cannot gnaw enough wood, his teeth will grow so fast they will grow right through his skull and kill him.

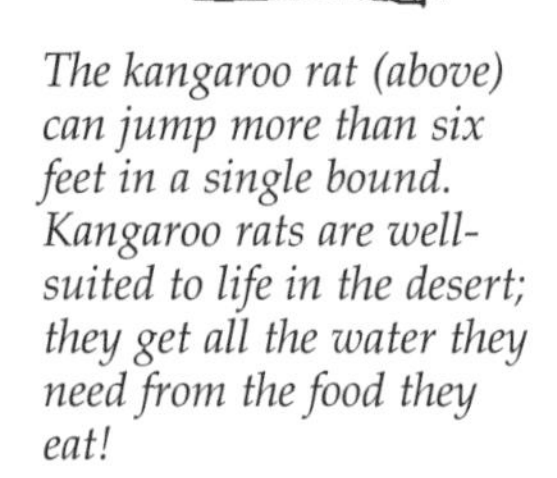

The kangaroo rat (above) can jump more than six feet in a single bound. Kangaroo rats are well-suited to life in the desert; they get all the water they need from the food they eat!

A muskrat (left) may have as many as thirty babies in a single year. Therefore, even though it is trapped extensively for its rich fur, it is in no danger of becoming extinct!

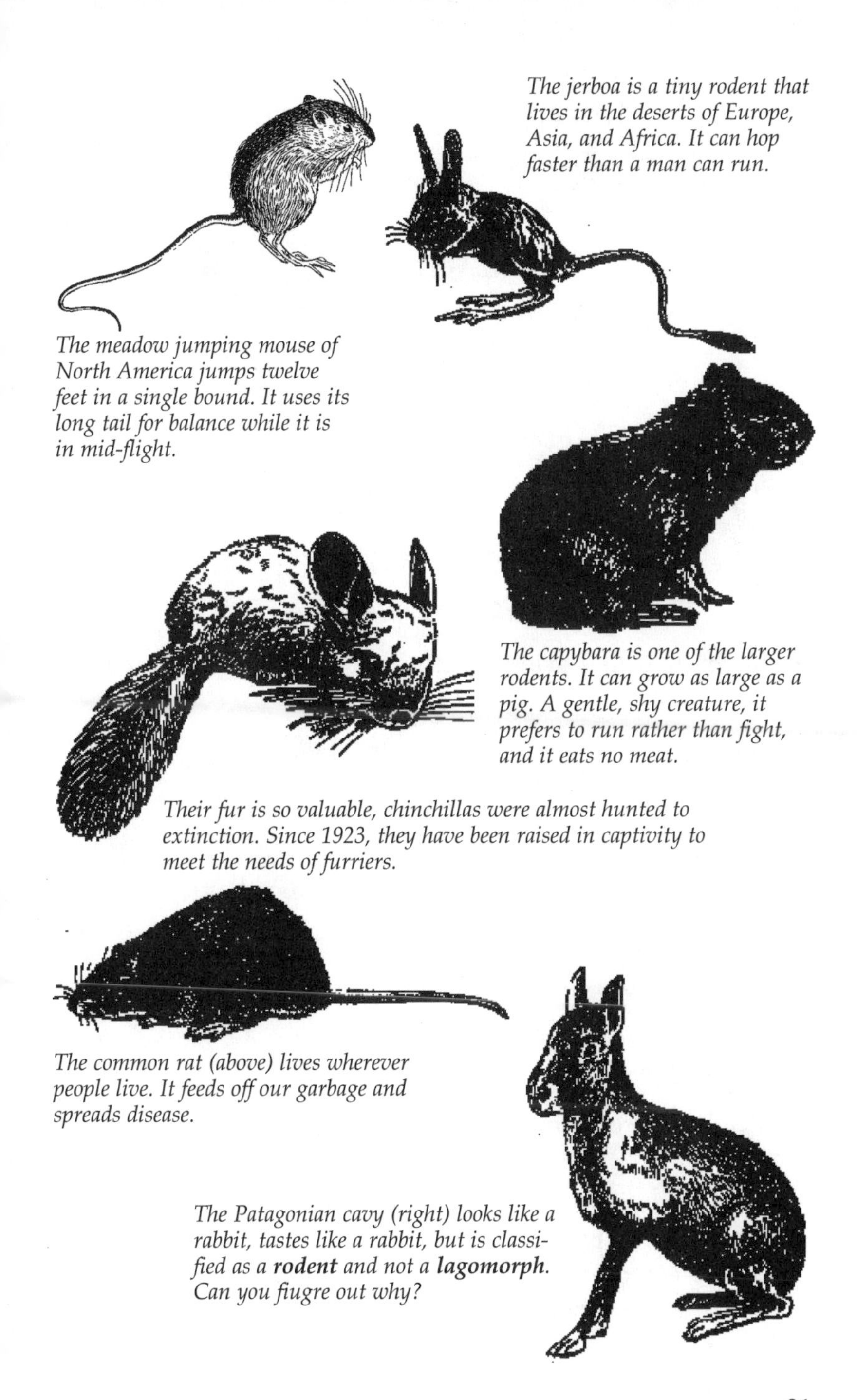

The jerboa is a tiny rodent that lives in the deserts of Europe, Asia, and Africa. It can hop faster than a man can run.

The meadow jumping mouse of North America jumps twelve feet in a single bound. It uses its long tail for balance while it is in mid-flight.

The capybara is one of the larger rodents. It can grow as large as a pig. A gentle, shy creature, it prefers to run rather than fight, and it eats no meat.

Their fur is so valuable, chinchillas were almost hunted to extinction. Since 1923, they have been raised in captivity to meet the needs of furriers.

The common rat (above) lives wherever people live. It feeds off our garbage and spreads disease.

The Patagonian cavy (right) looks like a rabbit, tastes like a rabbit, but is classified as a ***rodent*** *and not a* ***lagomorph****. Can you fiugre out why?*

*The flying squirrel (above right) is a regular squirrel with skin wings. The African scaly-tailed squirrel (above left) is pictured at rest and in mid-flight. Why are these squirrels classified as **rodents** and not **dermopteras**?*

Vocabulary

edentate – literally: having no teeth; functionally: having extremely weak teeth

lagomorph – hare-like, having the form of a hare

Questions

1. What are some of the distinguishing characteristics of the edentates? *(They have no – or very weak – teeth; they don't have incisors or canines; they do not maintain their body temperature as constant as other mammals do.)*
2. What are the two main categories of edentates? *(hairy and shelled)*
3. What are the most famous edentates? *(the sloth, the anteater, and the armadillo)*
4. A common name for pangolins is "scaly anteater." Besides having a very hard, scaly skin, how do pangolins differ from regular anteaters? *(They prefer ant eggs over the ants themselves.)*

5. What does aardvark mean in Dutch? *(earth pig)*
6. What are the three lagomorphs? *(hares, rabbits, and pikas)*
7. What one feature sets lagomorphs apart from all other mammals? *(They have two pairs of upper incisor teeth, one pair behind the other.)*
8. What are some of the differences between hares, rabbits, and pikas? *(Rabbits are born with very poor eyesight and without fur; hares have fur and good eyesight from birth; pikas, unlike hares and rabbits, have back legs that are almost the same length as their front legs; their ears are shorter and they are smaller all around than most rabbits and hares.)*
9. What is the largest order of mammals? *(rodents)*
10. What sets rodents apart from other animals? *(Their incisors always grow, and they must keep chewing or gnawing in order, partially, to keep the incisors from growing too long!)*
11. What are the three sub-orders of rodents? *(squirrel-like, mouse-like, and "other")*
12. The flying squirrel and the African scaly-tailed squirrel are both classified as rodents instead of dermopteras even though they have skin wings. Why? *(because they have rodent teeth)*
13. The Patagonian cavy sure looks like a hare (and doesn't lagomorph mean "having the form of a hare"?). So why is it a rodent and not a lagomorph? *(because it has rodent teeth)*

Order: Cetaceans (seh-TAY-shens)

The name cetacean comes from the Greek and Latin words for sea. The cetaceans are all the large, fishlike mammals: the dolphins, porpoises and whales.

While these animals look like fish, they are just as much mammals as any dogs, cats, or mice you may happen to know. The cetaceans are warm-blooded; they have lungs and breathe air; they bring forth their young alive; and most of all, they have mammary glands by which they feed their young. Fish, by contrast, are cold-blooded (meaning their blood temperature is controlled completely by their environment); they get their oxygen from water by means of gills; most hatch from eggs; and none have mammary glands. There is another difference between the cetaceans and fish: fish have tailfins, supported by bones, that run vertically; cetaceans' tails run horizontally and have no bones in them.

The blue, or sulphur-bottom whale is the largest animal that ever lived. It can grow as big as one hundred feet long and weigh as much as one hundred tons—200,000 pounds. That's twice as heavy as the heaviest dinosaur that ever lived!

The blue whale is the largest animal that ever lived. Though it lives in the sea, it is a true mammal. It is warm-blooded and nurses its young.

Even the sperm whale, the type of whale most sought after by whaling ships, grows to sixty feet or more in length. One forty-three foot sperm whale was weighed at 86,000 pounds—one ton for every foot of length!

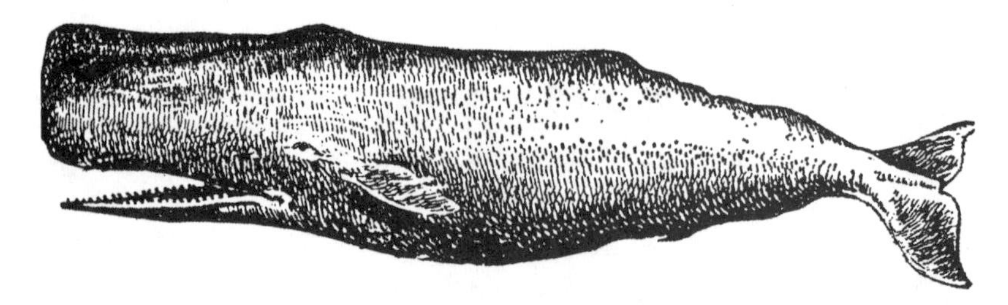

The sperm whale is highly prized for its oil. Notice its tail fins. Like all cetaceans the sperm whale's tail fins are horizontal rather than vertical.

When the fat from a sixty-foot sperm whale is boiled down, it can produce 4,000 gallons of oil.

Though we speak of three kinds of cetaceans, the dolphins, porpoises and whales, according to zoologists there are really only two: the toothed whales and the whalebone whales. The toothed whales have cone-shaped teeth in their mouths, which they use to catch and hold their prey. Toothed whales do not chew their food; they swallow it whole.

Dolphins and porpoises belong to the toothed whale group along with killer whales and sperm whales. Dolphins and porpoises differ in the shape of their heads; porpoises have rounded muzzles, dolphins have beaks. Both dolphins and porpoises are smaller than the other whales.

The common dolphin (top) and the bottlenose dolphin (bottom) have projecting beaks. Porpoises don't have beaks. Notice, too, that dolphins are toothed whales.

The sperm whale is the largest toothed whale. The sperm whale's head makes up one-third of its length. The head contains a huge reservoir filled with the whitish oily substance known as spermaceti (SPER-muh-SEH-tee). Scientists think that this oil acts as a cushion that somehow protects the whale's body from damage when it goes down to great depths. Sperm whales have been found as far as 3,200 feet below the surface of the ocean, where the pressure is 1,400 pounds to the square inch. They can stay at that depth for an hour or more.

The whalebone whales don't have teeth. Instead, they have curtains of baleen (buh-LEEN) or whalebone, that hang down from the roof of their mouth. One curtain hangs on each side of the mouth, and each curtain is made from thousands of individual strands of baleen.

When a whalebone whale opens its mouth, it gulps a huge amount of water . . . along with whatever plants or animals happen to be floating in that water. Once he has filled his mouth, the whale then closes it, and squirts the water back out through the baleen. The baleen acts as a strainer and allows the whale to keep whatever food he has found.

The large whales—which are the whalebone whales—can eat as much as a ton (2,000 pounds) of food in a day during the summer! During the winter they don't eat quite so much.

There are about 80 species of cetaceans.

The narwhal has a large, twisted tusk that juts out of its left, upper jaw. The narwhal itself may grow to twenty feet in length; its tusk can be nine feet long. Most scientists are agreed that the famous legends about unicorns were prompted by the discovery of narwhal tusks.

Vocabulary

cold-blooded—body temperature is controlled by the environment

spermaceti—an oily substance that fills a large reservoir in the heads of sperm whales; scientists think it helps protect the whale when it goes deep in the water

baleen—also known as whalebone; it hangs down in curtains in a whalebone whale's mouth; the whale uses it to strain food out of the water he brings into his mouth

Questions

1. What distinguishes cetaceans from fish? *(Fish are not mammals, cetaceans are [cetaceans breathe air using lungs, they are warm-blooded, bring forth their young live, have mammary glands, etc.]; also, cetaceans have tail fins that are horizontal and have no bones, while fish's tail fins are vertical and have bones.)*
2. How much food can a whalebone whale eat in a day? *(a ton – 2,000 pounds!)*
3. What are the three categories of cetaceans that most people recognize? *(porpoises, dolphins, and whales)*
4. What categories do scientists recognize? *(whalebone whales and toothed whales)*
5. What distinguishes toothed from whalebone whales? *(Toothed whales have teeth [!] while whalebone whales have baleen.)*
6. What is the biggest animal in the world – and how big can it get? *(The blue whale is biggest; it can grow to 100 feet in length and weigh 100 tons – 200,000 pounds!)*
7. How does baleen work? *(The whale sucks in a large amount of water, then spits it out after straining it through the baleen; the baleen catches the little creatures that are floating in the water.)*
8. Do toothed whales chew their food? *(no)*
9. How can you tell the difference between porpoises and dolphins? *(Porpoises have rounded snouts; dolphins have beaks.)*
10. Are porpoises and dolphins toothed whales or whalebone whales? *(toothed whales)*
11. What tend to be larger: toothed whales or whalebone whales? *(whalebone whales)*

Order: Carnivores

Carnivore means "meat eater."[9] In the same way that not all insectivores really eat insects, so, too, not all carnivores really eat meat. Still, the carnivores' teeth and claws make it appear as if they could all be meat-eaters.

There are six or seven families within the carnivores; these include the dog family; the bear family; the raccoon family; the musk family (weasels, minks, martens, polecats, sables, badgers, skunks, etc.); the hyena family; and the cat family (including everything from house cats to lions, tigers, cougars and lynxes).

There are about 250 species of carnivores.

CANIS—DOG FAMILY

The red or maned wolf lives in South America. Its long legs are perfect for running through tall grass.

The African or Cape dog roams in ferocious packs looking for animals to eat. Its favorite meal is antelope.

Reynard, the fox, is admired around the world for his cunning. Though hunted for being a chicken-killer, he also eats insects, mice, carrion (the bodies of dead animals), grass, and fruit.

---

[9]"Carn-" comes from the Latin word for "flesh" or "meat." Christians speak of the "in*carn*ation"—when Jesus took on the body of a man. He "in-fleshed" Himself. You can find the same root in the King James version of the Bible where some people are described as being "*carn*al" rather than "spiritual" (1 Corinthians 3:1-4). Modern translations substitute the word "fleshly" in place of the word "carnal."

Bear Family

The grizzly is named for its grey-tipped hair color, not for its ferocity. The grizzly is one of the more powreful land animals. American Spaniards at one time pitted grizzlies against bulls in the bullring. The grizzlies usually won.

At eight and a quarter feet in length, the polar bear is only slightly smaller than the Alaskan brown bear (nine feet long) – the world's largest meat-eating land animal. The polar bear lives in the far north and eats seals and walrus cubs.

The American black bear is the most common bear in North America. It grows to only five feet in length, but still weighs up to 500 pounds! It is a curious animal and will often raid human campsites.

Raccoon Family

Raccoons are sometimes known as the "bandits" of the animal world. This is partially because of the black mask on their face, partially because of their sneaking thievery. Raccoons are extremely fastidious; they always wash their food before they eat – even if the food is already clean!

The ring-tailed or red coati has the raccoon's face mask and a striped tail. But unlike North American raccoons, the coati has a long snout which it uses to hunt for birds and insects. A native of South America, the coati follows the Latin American tradition of taking afteroon siestas.

The kinkajou or "honey bear" is considered a raccoon but looks more like a New World monkey. It has a powerful, prehensile tail which it uses both to hang onto branches as well as to grab food that otherwise would be out of reach. The kinkajou enjoys eating fruit.

Zoologists say the panda is no bear but, rather, a member of the raccoon family. Its favorite food is bamboo shoots. It lives in the wilds of Tibet.

Musk Family

The members of the musk family have special glands that produce scented oils. The skunk is well known for its odor. Other musk animals are better known for other features.

The American badger (above) is a squat, heavy-bodied animal with large claws. If it feels endangered, it burrows underground. It cannot run quickly and is unable to climb trees.

You may have heard Rudyard Kipling's story of Rikki-tikki-tavi, the snake-killing mongoose. The mongoose really does kill snakes. It is a member of the musk family.

The wolverine (left) is the biggest member of this family and is tremendously ferocious. In Europe they called it the glutton because it seems to kill simply for the pleasure of killing.

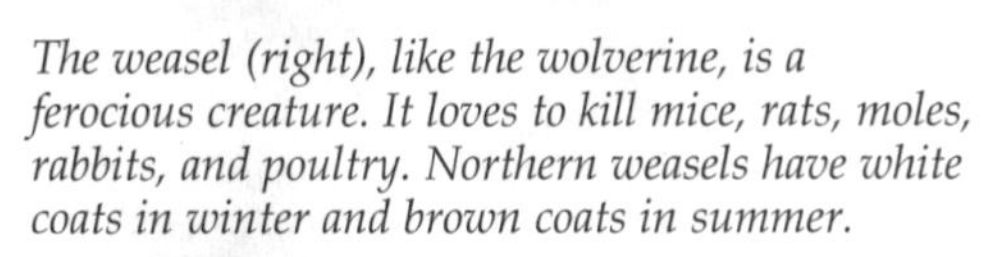

The weasel (right), like the wolverine, is a ferocious creature. It loves to kill mice, rats, moles, rabbits, and poultry. Northern weasels have white coats in winter and brown coats in summer.

Skunks (left) are most unpleasant to have around as long as they have their musk glands. When removed, however, they make a great pet. Perfumers sometimes use the musk oil from the skunk to make fine perfumes.

Hyena Family

A ruthless killer, the hyena (right) preys upon weak, old, or injured animals. Theodore Roosevelt once said he found a hyena stuck inside an elephant carcass – the hyena had eaten so much meat, it couldn't get back out the same hole it had used to get in.

The aardwolf (left) looks like a small hyena, but its character is completely different. It prefers to eat insects and when attacked, it bristles its mane and sprays a foul-smelling liquid just like the skunk does. "Aardwolf" is Dutch for "earth wolf." It gets its name from the fact that it lives in underground burrows.

Cat Family

The snow leopard (left) lives high above the timber line of the Himalayas. It has a soft, long-haired coat of pale gray or buff. It preys on mountain sheep, goats, hares, and other small game.

The Canadian lynx (right) has broad feet and strong legs that help it walk through snowy terrain but make it clumsy when it comes to running. Its long side whiskers give it a look of old-fashioned elegance. The lynx lives not only in Canada but in the northern United States as well.

The king of the jungle, the lion, is a family-oriented animal. It normally roams and hunts in family bands. If one lion makes a kill, it willingly shares with the rest of the pride. Lions generally leave people alone.

The tiger is as powerful as the lion but far more bloodthirsty. It prefers life by itself. The tiger can climb, jump, and, unlike most cats, even swim.

The jaguar (below) lives in North and South America. It looks a lot like a leopard, but has a larger head and a heavier body. The spots in its coat are also larger than the leopard's. The jaguar prefers fish, peccaries, sloths, and capybaras.

The cheetah is the fastest land animal. At top speed it can hit seventy miles per hour. Though in many ways a cat, the cheetah has the legs and non-retracting claws of a dog.

Order: Pinnipeds or "Finfeet"

The pinnipeds, or "finfeet," are often counted among the carnivores; sometimes they are given their own class. They are true meat eaters. The pinnipeds eat lots of fish, but they also like to eat other sea animals such as squids and shellfish.

Sea lions, walruses and seals are all pinnipeds.

Unlike cetaceans, pinnipeds do not live their entire lives in the sea. In fact, they spend quite a bit of time lounging on land.

All pinnipeds have finned flippers. They are slower swimmers than cetaceans, but they can maneuver themselves much more easily than can the cetaceans. The pinnipeds live very happily in the pounding surf near jagged rocks.

There are about 20 species of pinnipeds.

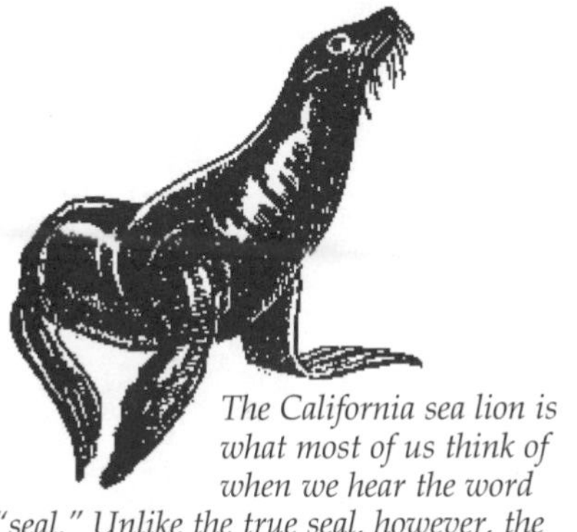

The California sea lion is what most of us think of when we hear the word "seal." Unlike the true seal, however, the sea lion has small external ears and has hind limbs that can be pointed forward to help it move about on dry land.

The walrus is a huge animal – up to twelve feet long and 3,000 pounds. With its long (up to 39-inch) tusks, it defends itself against polar bears and killer whales. It also uses its tusks to pry shellfish from the bottom of the ocean and to pull itself up on land.

The elephant seal is the largest seal and can weigh more than 5,000 pounds. It has an astonishing nose – sometimes over nine inches long.

True seals have no outside ear, and their rear flippers stick straight out in back. They are covered with fur. The Alaskan ribbon seal (pictured) is a true seal.

Order: Sea Cows

Sea cows include the dugongs and the manatees. Though the sea cows all look like pinnipeds on the outside, the insides of their bodies are quite different, and they eat differently. They are strict vegetarians (while the pinnipeds are carnivores).

There are four species of sea cows.

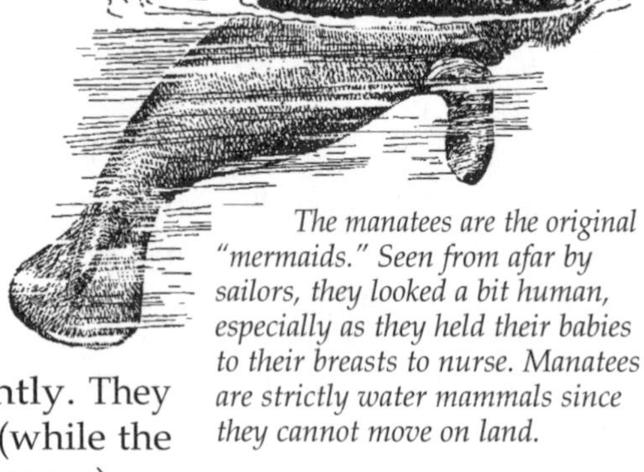

The manatees are the original "mermaids." Seen from afar by sailors, they looked a bit human, especially as they held their babies to their breasts to nurse. Manatees are strictly water mammals since they cannot move on land.

Vocabulary

carnivore – literally: "meat-eater"

Questions

1. What are the six main families of carnivores? *(dogs, bears, raccoons, musks, hyenas, and cats)*
2. Since not all carnivores eat meat (and they don't!), why are they called carnivores? *(Because their body structures – their teeth and claws, especially – make them look as if they should eat meat.)*
3. What is the primary difference between sea cows and pinnipeds? *(Sea cows are strict vegetarians; pinnipeds are meat-eaters.)*

Order: Elephants

Most of us know what an elephant is. It has many unique features: a long "trunk" formed from its nose and upper lip; huge ears; enlarged teeth in its upper jaws that stick forward to make tusks; and a thick, leathery hide. At one time, there were many species of elephants including huge, woolly mammoths that roamed the far north regions of the world, and a small elephant, no bigger than a pony, that lived in the Mediterranean.

Nowadays there are just three living species of elephants.

The male bush elephant (right) can stand twelve feet tall at the shoulder and weigh over twelve thousand pounds (six tons). The Asian elephant (left) is quite a bit smaller and can be recognized by its distinctively smaller ears and pointed head. The Asian elephant is especially valued for its ability to carry heavy loads (up to two thousand pounds, though usually no more than six hundred pounds) and to drag even heavier loads (up to four thousand pounds).

Order: Hyraxes

The rock hyrax, known as a coney in the Bible, enjoys lying out in the sun. Its worst enemy is the wild dog.

The hyraxes live in Africa, the Middle East and into Asia. They are small creatures, about the size of rabbits. They are vegetarians and their teeth look like the teeth of rhinoceroses (though, of course, much smaller!).

The hyraxes' feet are designed somewhat similar to those of elephants. They have four toes that end in blunt claws that look a lot like hoofs. The soles of hyraxes' feet are naked (they have no hair), but they are well padded.

The Bible mentions the Syrian hyrax or Daman in three places—Leviticus 11:5, Deuteronomy 14:7, and Psalm 104:18. Our translations call them "conies."

There are seven species of hyrax in the world today.

Order: Odd-Toed Ungulates

The Asian wild ass (left) roams the Asian deserts in large bands. Though curious about people, it keeps its distance. The donkeys we know come from African stock.

The African hook-lipped rhinoceros can run at thirty miles per hour or faster! It eats leaves, twigs, and the shoots of herbs and grasses.

Looking very much like a striped donkey, the zebra's stripes help it hide from lions when wandering in grassy surroundings. Besides its stripes, however, the zebra relies on its keen hearing and sense of smell.

The tapir is another "committee" animal with the body of a large pig, an oversized nose, and a head that seems a cross between an elephant and a rhinoceros. The Malay tapir has fur that is almost perfectly divided between gray and black.

Odd-toed ungulates (UNG-gue-lits) have either one or three toes (an odd number—that's where "odd-toed" comes from) on each foot that touch the ground. The word ungulate means "having hoofs." Odd-toed ungulates, then, are hoofed animals with one or three toes that touch the ground. They include three families: the equus or horse family: the horses, asses and zebras; the tapirs; and the rhinoceroses. All of these animals bear the weight of their bodies on their middle toes.

There are about 20 species of odd-toed ungulates.

Order: Even-Toed Ungulates

Knowing what an odd-toed ungulate is, you can probably figure out what an even-toed ungulate is.

An even-toed ungulate is a hoofed animal that has either two or four toes per foot. Even-toed ungulates bear their weight between their middle toes.

The even-toed ungulates include three main families: 1) the "normal-stomach" animals—the pig family: pigs, peccaries, and hippopotamuses; 2) the cud-chewers[10] with incisor and canine teeth—the camel family; and 3) all the cud-chewing animals that lack upper front teeth. This family is broken down into sub-families: the deer, giraffes, and pronghorns; the oxen (bison, cattle, yaks, and other oxen); the antelopes; the goats and sheep; and the goat-antelopes (neither goat nor antelope but much like both).

Scripture teaches us that many of the even-toed ungulates should be classified together. In Leviticus 11:3ff God tells the Israelites that they are allowed to eat any animals that chew the cud and have hoofs "completely split through." They are not allowed, however, to eat those that have split hoofs but do not chew the cud or those that chew the cud but have hoofs not completely divided.

There are about 190 species of even-toed ungulates.

---

[10]"Cud" is food that has been chewed once, swallowed, and regurgitated. Animals that "chew the cud" have a special system of three and sometimes four stomachs.

THE PIG FAMILY

. . . includes a wide range of animals from the true pig to the peccary (below left), to the wild boar (middle), to the warthog (right), and even the hippopotamus!

THE CAMEL FAMILY

. . . includes the dromedary, or one-humped camels of the mid-east, the Bactrian, or two-humped camels of Asia, and the alpacas, guanacos (below left), llamas, and vicuñas of South America.

Vocabulary

mammal—having mammary glands that produce milk to feed their young; warm-blooded, hairy, never more than two pairs of limbs, reproduce sexually

cud—food that has been chewed once, swallowed, and regurgitated

vore (as in insectivore, carnivore, voracious, devour)—to eat

carn- (as in carnivore, incarnation, carnal)—meat

THE GIRAFFE SUB-FAMILY

. . . stands by itself. Literally. Giraffes can grow to nineteen feet, the tallest land animals by far. Despite their long necks, giraffes have no more vertebrae (neck bones) than you or I!

THE DEER SUB-FAMILY

. . . includes everything from the moose (right) with antlers that, on their own, can extend six feet across and weigh sixty pounds, to the Chilean pudu (immediately below the moose) that stands no more than thirteen and a half inches high at the shoulders and weighs only up to twenty-four pounds.

Also pictured here (continuing clockwise around the group) are the European fallow deer (the kind Robin Hood would have shot), the polar caribou (wild reindeer), and the American elk.

THE OXEN/CATTLE SUB-FAMILY

. . . includes all the buffalo, oxen, and beef animals. Below are pictured the Asian water buffalo or carabao (left) and the Tibetan yak or grunting ox. At the top of page 110 you can see pictures of an African Cape, or black, buffalo (with the widespread horns), a heavy-maned American bison, and a comparatively well-groomed European bison.

THE PRONGHORN SUB-FAMILY
. . . members are like the sheep, goats, and antelope in that their horns are hollow. Yet, unlike these other animals, and similar to deer, the pronghorns shed their horns once each year. Both males and female pronghorns have horns.

THE ANTELOPE SUB-FAMILY
. . . includes a number of fleet-footed animals. Among them: the African gnu or wildebeest (below left), the eland (middle), and the greater kudu (below right).

THE GOAT-ANTELOPE SUB-FAMILY
Seemingly half-goat, half-antelope, the goat-antelopes include the so-called musk ox (below left) and the Rocky Mountain goat. The musk ox is not an ox, and the Rocky Mountain goat is not a goat.

Questions

1. What order of mammals has more kinds than all the others combined? *(rodents)*
2. What are the three families of odd-toed ungulates? *(horses, tapirs, and rhinoceroses)*
3. Can you remember the families of even-toed ungulates? *(pigs, camels, and cud-chewers lacking upper front teeth)*
4. What are the primary sub-families of even-toed ungulates? *(deer, giraffes, pronghorns; oxen/cattle; antelopes; goats/sheep; and goat-antelopes)*
5. Have someone read the names of each one of the nineteen orders of mammals. See if you can name one important characteristic of each order and give an example of a specific animal that is part of that order:

monotreme
insectivore
chiroptera
edentate
aardvark
rodent
carnivore
sea cow
hyrax
even-toed ungulate
marsupial
dermoptera
primate
pangolin
lagomorph
cetacean
pinniped
elephant
odd-toed ungulate

Class: Birds

Biologists figure there are about 8,600 species of birds in the world. They come in all different shapes, sizes and habits. Scientists put them in orders based on their habits and body forms.

Typical Characteristics

- One thing sets **birds** apart from all other animals: birds have feathers. No other animals have feathers, and no birds lack feathers. There are a few birds whose feathers are different from what we are used to—for instance, penguin feathers are hard and small, and the cassowary of Papua-New Guinea has feathers that are long, hard, and sharp—but all birds have feathers.
- Besides feathers, all birds have wings, though they don't all use their wings to fly. The ostrich, for instance, uses its wings to help it balance as it runs along at something like 40 miles per hour. The penguin, on the other hand, uses its wings like flippers when it goes for a swim in the ocean. (The penguin doesn't fly, either.)
- All birds are oviparous: they hatch from eggs.
- All birds are warm-blooded.
- Birds do not have teeth.
- Birds care for their young when they are first born.

The ostrich is the largest modern bird. At over seven feet tall and having good eyesight, it is able to see danger from afar and, though unable to fly, its long legs allow it to travel at 40 miles per hour. Ostriches are the only birds with just two toes.

The largest modern bird is the ostrich, which can grow up to eight feet tall and weigh up to three hundred pounds. The bee hummingbird is the smallest bird. It measures only two inches long when it is full grown and weighs a mere one-tenth of an ounce (about as much as half a sheet of regular typing paper)!

There are almost thirty orders of birds. We will not study the orders themselves, but will look at some of the variety God has built into all the birds.

Order: Ratites

. . . are the birds with flat breastbones. ("Ratite" means "raft" — which is a flat-bottomed boat.) The **ratites** include most of the flightless birds: the ostriches, emus, kiwis, penguins, rheas, moas (now extinct), cassowaries, and so forth. Birds that fly need a "keeled" breastbone so that their wing muscles have a place to which they can be attached. Without this keel, the ratites have wings too weak to enable them to fly.

Unable to fly, penguins waddle, weave, and toboggan on the snow and ice, but they are excellent swimmers.

The Kiwi, a ratite, lays eggs that are one-fourth its own weight – by far the largest bird egg in proportion to the size of the adult. Unlike other birds, the Kiwi has a very good sense of smell.

Order: Swimming, Diving, and Water Birds

. . . are those that get their food from the water. These include the loons, grebes, albatrosses, petrels, pelicans, swans, geese, ducks and screamers. These birds make up at least five different orders. Zoologists divide them based on the shape of their beaks, the structure of their

The albatross can have a wingspread up to twelve feet across. It lives at sea its entire life except when it breeds.

The loon (left), though helpless on land, is a magnificent swimmer and diver. In fact, it is able to outswim fish – which is how it gets its meals. The loon's cry sounds like a madman's laugh; hence the phrase "craxy as a loon."

The pelican (right) has a large pouch under its bill in which it stores the fish it catches. When the pelican chicks want food, they poke around in their mother's pouch until they find something they want. Pelicans can grow to five feet in length with a wingspan of seven feet.

feet, how and where they catch their food, and other characteristics. Some of these birds have webbed feet; some have separate toes. Some get around just fine on land. Loons' legs, however, are set so far back on their bodies that they cannot balance themselves to walk.

Order: Wading Birds

. . . come from two orders. All of the birds in these groups have long legs. They include flamingos, herons, ibises, storks, and others.

The spoonbill's (above) bill widens out at the tip so it is wider than the bird's head! The spoonbill uses its wonderful bill to strain small snails, insects, and other delicacies out of the water.

By stretching its neck and holding its head almost upside down, the flamingo (right) is able to sift its food from bottom mud. Its favorite food is shellfish.

The avocet's (left) long bill is different because it curves upward. Both parents tend the eggs until the chicks hatch. Avocets can usually be found in the company of the stilt, a bird that has the longest legs in proportion to its size.

Order: Shore Birds

. . . run along the water's edge, but often feed from the ocean. The shore birds include all the gulls, auks, plovers, sandpipers, and others.

The Atlantic puffin (left) has a big black head, an oversized blue and crimson bill, white under parts, and red legs. Add to this its clumsy waddle and harsh cloak, and you have the clown of the bird world.

The golden plover (right) spends its summers in Alaska and its winters in Hawaii. It makes the 2,400-mile trip between its two homes twice a year. It makes no stops along the way.

The black-backed gull (right) is the largest sea gull – more than two and a half feet long and with a wingspread of five and a half feet.

Order: Daytime Birds of Prey

Falcons, eagles, hawks, condors, ospreys, and several other birds are called daytime **birds of prey**. They attack and eat all kinds of animals—from other birds, to small mammals, to fish, insects, snakes and other reptiles.

The peregrine falcon (above) may be the world's fastest bird. It has been clocked at up to 180 mph when diving for prey.

The secretary bird (left) is a champion snake-killer on the flatlands of Africa. Ranchers often tame the birds to acquire their reptile and rodent-killing services.

Order: Fowls

Chickens, pheasants, grouse, turkeys, peacocks and many other birds make up the order of fowls. All of these birds scratch in the dirt for their food. They tend to be vegetarians, but some also like to fill up on insects.

Turkeys were eaten by Aztecs long before Europeans ever came to America. The wild turkey (right) can grow three feet tall and has a wingspread of over three feet.

Order: Tree-Hole Dwellers

Woodpeckers, toucans, puffbirds and many others have wonderful feet for climbing and digging in wood: two of their toes point forward, and two point back. This gives them a great grip on the trees in which they make their homes!

The toucan (above) has a bill so large, the bird makes special arrangements when it goes to sleep. First it turns its head backward and lays it sidewise on top of its back, then it spreads its tail like a fan and folds it over its bill and back. Now it is ready for sleep!

Woodpeckers (left) have chisel-shaped bills, a specially designed head to protect them while they peck, and powerful feet to get a strong grip on the tree they are pecking.

Order: Perching Birds

The largest number of birds—about 60 different "families" and 5,100 species, more than half of all the different bird species—are perching birds. Perching birds have four toes—three pointing forward and one back—and sit in trees. About 4,000 species of perching birds are also called **song birds** based on the sounds they make.

The bird of paradise (male and female, above left), the barn swallow (above middle), and the raven (above right) are just a few members of the order of ***perching birds****.*

Order: Pigeons

Pigeons form their own order. Of course you've seen the common pigeons, the pigeons that inhabit almost every city of the world. The pigeon to the right, the crowned pigeon, is the world's largest. It lives in Papua New Guinea, an island nation just north of Australia.

Order: Parrots

Parrots also have their own order.

The macaw (left) is one of the most brilliantly colored parrots. It can crack a Brazil nut (a large, hard-shelled nut) with its bill!

Order: Cuckoos

Cuckoos make a two-tone sound that starts high and ends low: "Coo-coo!"

The road runner (right) is a cuckoo. The road runner's favorite food is lizards, but it also eats snails after smashing them against rocks. People in the southwest United States and Mexico appreciate road runners for their ability to kill rattlesnakes.

Order: Nighttime Birds of Prey

. . . is made up of all the owls.

The great horned owl (right) is so fierce, it has been known to drive eagles from their nests! God has made owls a bit like stealth bombers, only instead of scattering radar waves, owls have lots of downy feathers to scatter sound. Unlike other birds, they are able to dive on their prey without being heard.

Order: Nighttime Insect Eaters

. . . consists of birds that have large mouths and small beaks. They eat somewhat the way whalebone whales eat: they hold their mouths open as they fly allowing their mouths to catch whatever insects may happen to be in their way.

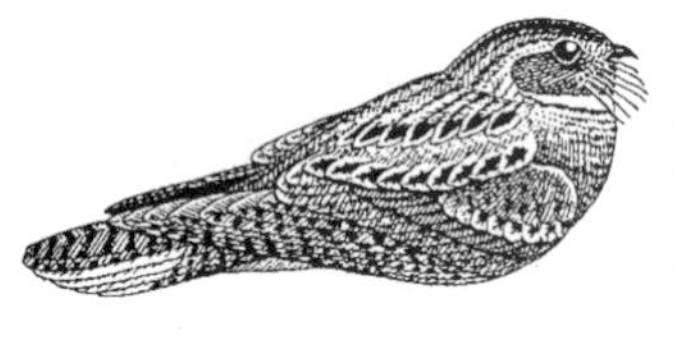

The whippoorwill is a typical nighttime insect eater with a large mouth and small beak. It has a stunning call that sounds just like its name: "whippoorwill!" One ornithologist (a person who studies birds) counted more than 400 calls in a row!

Order: "No-Foot" Birds

. . . includes hummingbirds and swifts that have strong wings and extremely weak feet so they fly almost constantly.

Hummingbirds include the smallest and some of the most beautifully colored members of the bird phylum. Hummingbirds are also noted for their ability to fly backwards! Among the members of this order are the Gould's hummingbird (top) and the ruby-throated hummingbird (lower left) which is supposed to be able to fly at up to 55 mph.

Order: Trogons

. . . includes birds with long tails and weak feet that eat fruit and live in the tropics.

The sacred bird of the Aztecs, the quetzal (right), is a trogon. It is highly prized for its beautiful colors: green, scarlet, black, and white. Its brilliant green tail is close to two feet long!

Order: Birds with Fused Toes

. . . includes the hoopoes, kingfishers and others.

The kookaburra, or laughing jackass (above left), is a member of the kingfisher family. It eats crabs, rats, mice, and reptiles. The hoopoe (right) looks like it might be an American Indian chief, but it comes from the Old World. Its favorite food is ants, which it gets at by means of its long, curved bill. The hornbill family has many members but the rhinoceros hornbill (middle) has probably the most interesting bill shape. From the tip of the bill to the tip of the tail, these birds can grow as long as six feet!

Bird Characteristics

As we have seen, zoologists sort birds according to their physical features and according to their habits.

So that you can look at birds a little more wisely, we show here just a few design features you might look for.

Feet and Beaks

On the following page are some different kinds of birds' feet and beaks. A bird's feet can tell you about how that bird lives. For example, birds that catch prey, such as mice, for their dinner will have different kinds of feet from birds that must hold onto the trunk of a tree and peck for insects.

Look at each of the pictures, and think: What kind of feet does this bird have? How many toes does it have? How does the bird use its feet?

Then ask similar questions for each of the beaks or bills shown. What kind of bill does the bird have? What shape is it? What does the bird do with it? How does the bird use it?

Vocabulary

bird—warm-blooded, has feathers, has wings, oviparous, cares for its young

ratite—"raft-shaped"—i.e., flat—breast bone; flightless bird

bird of prey—bird that attacks and eats animals

song bird—a type of perching bird that is known for its voice

Questions

1. What kinds of food do the fowls eat? *(Food that is found in the dirt, whether pieces of vegetation or small insects.)*

2. How do the nighttime insect-eating birds' mouths and bills help them to eat? *(Their mouths are big [even though their beaks are small], so as they fly along, they keep their mouths open so that their mouths will tend to scoop insects out of the air.)*
3. What other animal feeds somewhat like the nighttime insect-eating birds? *(**baleen** or **whalebone whales**)*
4. How do the tree-hole dwelling birds' feet help them? *(They are designed to grab onto wood, whether facing up or down the tree.)*

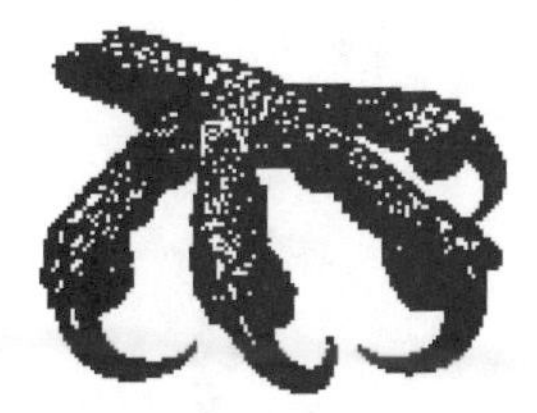

Grasping Foot *– used by birds of prey to catch and hold animals. Notice the large, curved claws!*

Webbed Foot *– used by swimming birds to help propel them through the water.*

Clinging Foot *– used by tree-hole dwellers to hang onto the tree while they peck or climb.*

Scratching Foot *– used by fowls to pry seeds and insects out of hard-packed soil.*

Running Foot *– notice that all toes point forward and the claws are short.*

Perching Foot *– used by perching birds to hang onto the branches where they sit. The hind toe curls behind the branch.*

5. How do the feet of birds of prey help them? *(They have sharp curved talons, or claws, that help them grasp their prey.)*
6. How did God design swimming birds' feet to help them swim? *(The webbing between the toes gives them additional surface area to push water and so propel them along.)*

***Probing Bill** – brown creepers can use their sharp-pointed bills to discover insects in the bark of trees.*

***Chisel Bill** – woodpeckers use their hard, sharp bills to detect insects inside wood, and then to dig the insects out.*

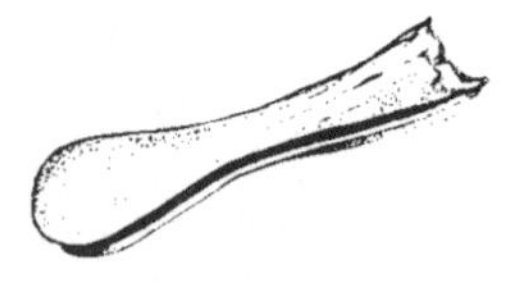

***Detecting Bill** – spoonbills sweep their bills through the water until they bump against something . . . at which point they know they have found some prey!*

***Scooping Bill** – water birds often have bills that do a good job of scooping up fish.*

***Trapping Bill/Mouth** – the kind nighttime insect eaters have: great for scooping up insects one happens to run into!*

***Cracking Bill** – used by many seed- and nut-eaters like the parrots.*

Class: Amphibians

Amphibians are animals that live part of their lives in water and part of their lives on dry land. There are only three orders of amphibians. They are the frogs, the salamanders and the caecilians (seh-SILL-yens).

1. Most amphibians hatch from eggs laid in the water. When they first hatch, they are called larvae (LAR-vee or LAR-vay; plural of larva [LAR-vuh]). Frog, toad and salamander larvae are called tadpoles or polliwogs. These larvae breathe using gills.

2. At a certain point, the larvae's bodies begin to change in a process called metamorphosis. In those amphibians that will have lungs, their gills are slowly replaced by lungs; frog, toad and salamander larvae grow legs.

3. Metamorphosis can take from two weeks to several months but eventually, once the changes are complete, most amphibians have to leave the water in which they were born and live on land.

4. Amphibians are cold-blooded. They use almost none of the energy from their food in order to heat their bodies.

5. Amphibians' skin has no hair, scales, or feathers.

6. Amphibians' skin is always moist. It is made moist by special glands beneath the skin's surface. Instead of sweat (like mammals), these glands secrete mucus. It is this mucus that causes amphibians to feel slimy when touched.

In the same way that the evaporation of sweat on your body helps your body cool down when you are hot, the evaporation of the mucus on amphibians' skin causes amphibians to be cooler than the air around them.

The skin mucus is good for something else besides keeping amphibians cool. It also enables them to absorb oxygen through their skin! They can "breathe" through their skin, if you will!

Most amphibians get most of the oxygen they need when they are adults by means of lungs and gills when they are immature. But some amphibians have both lungs and gills, and there are a few kinds of salamanders that have neither lungs nor gills. All the oxygen they need comes through the mucus on their skins and through the mucus membranes in their mouths and throats!

Unlike most other animals, amphibians do not drink water. They get the water they need by absorbing it through their skin—either by plopping themselves in some water or by sitting on or in moist dirt. Humid air does not have enough moisture in it to meet amphibians' water needs.

Amphibians lay a lot of eggs—hundreds and sometimes even thousands. Remember that the word for "egg-laying" is oviparous. Unlike birds' eggs, amphibians' eggs don't have shells. Instead, they are surrounded by a protective jelly. Most kinds of amphibian parents do not care for their children once they are born.

Amphibians live around the world, from the tip of South America in the south to the Arctic Circle in the north. Only about forty species are known in Europe, about 300 in the United States. Most are in the tropical regions. In fact, one author says "the Amazon basin of South America and the Cameroons in Africa are teeming with frogs, in such numbers that it may be years before all the kinds living there are found and classified."[11]

Order: Frogs

The frog order, consisting of both frogs and toads, has by far the most members—almost 2,700 species. When they are adults, frogs and toads have four legs and no tail. Frogs' and toads' hind legs are longer than their front legs and are extremely powerful for jumping. Even though, as a group, all tailless amphibians are members of the "frogs" order, zoologists distinguish between toads and frogs. Toads, they say, usually have

The American Bullfrog (left) is the largest tailless amphibian in the United States. Females, which are larger than males, grow to eight inches in length. They lay about 20,000 eggs at a time.

American toads (right) have been known to travel back to their breeding sites even when carried more than a mile away.

[11]Goodwin, op. cit., 1193.

rough skin that is moist but not slippery wet. Frogs, by contrast, are comparatively smooth-skinned and have a much wetter feel.

Order: Salamanders

There are about 330 species of salamanders. Adult salamanders have a long tail and four short, weak legs.[12]

Salamanders use their legs for walking on land, and their tails for moving in the water. Most salamanders live in the temperate areas of the world—places where, when the seasons change, the temperature changes as well. Some also live in the tropical areas of South and Central America. The smallest salamander is barely two inches long; the largest, the Japanese giant salamander, grows to five feet!

Salamanders are one of the only kinds of animals that can regrow limbs if they are cut off. They can regrow their tails and even their legs!

More salamanders live in North America (including Mexico) than any other place in the world. There are no salamanders in Australia and only three species in Africa.

The arboreal (tree) salamander has no lungs. Instead, it gets the oxygen it needs through its skin and the mucus membranes in its mouth and throat.

Order: Caecilians

You've probably never seen a caecilian before. There are about 150 species of caecilians in the world. They look like long earthworms or very skinny snakes. They have no legs and they live in the

---

[12]Two salamanders that spend their entire lives in the water have only two front legs.

tropics. Most are less than twelve inches long, but one grows to as much as five feet in length!

Caecilians are different from the other amphibians in that they don't undergo the same kinds of body changes that frogs, toads and salamanders experience. They often spend their entire lives either in underground burrows or in water.

Vocabulary

larva—a newly hatched amphibian baby before it has undergone metamorphosis

metamorphosis—the process of a complete change in body structures or functions—such as when a tadpole turns into a frog: it loses its tail, grows legs, and gills become lungs

tadpole—another name for a frog, toad, or salamander larva

polliwog—same meaning as tadpole

lungs—organs that permit oxygen to get into an animal's body from the *air*

gills—organs that permit oxygen to get into an animal's body from *water*

mucus—a slimy secretion of the body

mucous membrane—the part of an animal's body that produces mucus

cold-blooded—getting body heat from the environment rather than from food

Questions

1. How do amphibian eggs differ from bird eggs? *(They don't have shells; instead, they are surrounded by a jelly.)*

2. What makes an amphibian an amphibian? *(It has no hair; has wet skin [from mucus, not sweat]; it is oviparous, hatching from a jelly-coated, rather than a shelled egg; when it is first born, its body is in a different form from what it will be when it is an adult.*[13]*)*

3. What happens to amphibians during metamorphosis? *(Their bodies change form; polliwogs and tadpoles grow lungs and lose their gills; they also lose their tails and grow legs.)*

4. How can you tell the difference between a frog and a toad? *(A frog has relatively smooth skin and a wet feel; a toad generally has bumpy skin and a dryer feel.)*

5. What two things do amphibians' mucus glands do for them? *(They produce mucus which keeps amphibians cool, and gives them a little more oxygen.)*

6. What can salamanders do that only a few other animals can? *(They can regrow body parts.)*

7. What can some salamanders do that no other animals can? *(They can breathe without lungs or gills; they breathe through their skin and other mucus membranes!)*

Class: Reptiles

There are four main orders of reptiles: the crocodilians, the snakes and lizards, the turtles, and an animal called the tuatara (too-uh-TAR-uh). Altogether, the reptiles include close to 6,000 species.

---

[13]When humans are born our bodies, though much *smaller* than they will become, have the same *form* as they will have once we are grown. When we are born we normally have two legs, two arms, one head, one mouth, one nose, two eyes, two ears, and so on. When we grow up, we have the same number of all of these organs, and they have much the same shape they had when we were born. This is different from amphibians whose gills will metamorphose (change form) and become lungs, whose tails will disappear, or whose bodies will grow legs that weren't there when they first hatched. . . .

How You Can Distinguish Reptiles from Other Animals

1. Reptiles have dry, scaly skin.
2. They breathe by means of lungs.
3. They are cold-blooded.
4. Most reptiles have very good sight. Species that are active during the day usually have round pupils; those that are active at night usually have slit-shaped pupils. (The reason for the slit shape, apparently, is to permit the eye to block out most sunshine during the day.)
5. Many reptiles molt. That means, as they grow, new scales grow under their old ones. Eventually, the old skin breaks apart and falls off.

Reptiles use three different methods to reproduce. Most are oviparous; they are hatched from eggs. An egg-hatched baby has no physical connection to its mother while it is in the egg.

A few reptiles are viviparous (vih-VIH-per-us). **Viviparous** means "born alive." Viviparous babies come out of their mothers fully formed, ready to get along pretty much on their own. These reptiles have a placental system very similar to most mammals. While the eggs are still inside the mother, the shell disappears so that the mother can be attached to the growing babies.

Finally, some reptiles are **ovoviviparous** (OH-voh-vih-VIH-per-us), meaning they begin inside an egg, inside the mother. But, the mother never lays the egg! When the baby hatches from its egg, it hatches inside its mother's body. After it hatches, then it is born!

Reptile eggs are generally tough-shelled. If a reptile is oviparous, it lays its eggs on land.

Pythons, mudsnakes and some skinks (legless lizards) will protect their eggs until they hatch. Alligator mothers will carry their babies to water once they hatch from their eggs. Otherwise reptiles don't do much of anything to care for their young.

Pythons are the longest reptiles alive today. Some grow as long as 30 feet. But pythons are by no means the heaviest reptiles. The biggest pythons may weigh only 400 pounds. The heaviest reptiles are sea turtles (one weighed over 1,500 pounds) and crocodiles (some have been estimated to weigh 2,000 pounds).

Order: Crocodilians

There are about twenty-five known species of crocodilians. The crocodilians look like giant lizards except they have long snouts, strong jaws, and webbed hind feet. The crocodilians include the crocodiles, of course, but also the alligators, caimans, and gavials. All four types of animal look similar.

The gavials have long, slender snouts and live in the rivers of India and Burma, in south and southeast Asia. Crocodiles are found in warm areas worldwide. Most alligators live in the Americas; one species is found in China. Caimans are a kind of alligator that lives in the tropical Americas.

You can tell the difference between a crocodile and an alligator by the way their snouts and teeth are formed. Both alligators and crocodiles have several teeth in their bottom jaws that are larger than the rest. When a crocodile closes its mouth, you can still see these teeth because they stick out on the sides of the upper jaw. An alligator's large teeth fit into grooves inside his mouth. When he closes his mouth, you won't be able to see his teeth.

Another difference between the two animals may be seen in the snout: alligators' snouts are more rounded than crocodiles' snouts. If you were going to tell the difference based on snout shape, however, you would probably have to look at quite a few of both kinds of animal. And to be honest, I think I'd rather keep my distance. If one of them happened to catch your leg, he could snap it in two with a single chomp of his jaw.

The crocodilians' skin grows in large segments called plates.

Order: Lizards and Snakes

There are more than 6,200 species of lizards and snakes—about 2,400 species of snakes and 3,800 species of lizards.

You would think snakes and lizards should be put in different orders: most lizards have four legs; snakes have none. Lizards have eyelids; snakes have none. Lizards have ear openings on the outsides of their heads; snakes have none. And lizards generally have far fewer vertebrae than the snakes do. Despite these differences, most biologists cling to the idea that snakes and lizards are close relatives (in other words: that they evolved from a common ancestor)!

The marine iguana is almost three feet long. It is one of the rare reptiles that actually swims.

The Gila (HEE-luh) monster (right) grows to about two feet in length. It has a bite that is as poisonous as a rattlesnake's.

The crested lizard or desert iguana may have a body temperature as high as 110°F. It is a favorite dinner for sidewinder rattlesnakes.

Lizards' tails are usually at least as long as their bodies. The so-called glass snake (one of the few legless lizards) has a tail that is twice as long as its body. Snakes' tails, however, are only a fraction as long—perhaps a tenth (or less) the length of the rest of the snake's body.

Many lizards are like salamanders in their ability to regrow their tails if their tails are cut off. (Snakes cannot regrow their tails.)

Some lizards also have the ability to change their colors depending on their environment. If they are sitting on a brown stone, they will take on the same coloration; if they are sitting on a green leaf, they will turn green.

Lizards that can change their color don't always color themselves the same color as their background. If they feel cold, they will sometimes darken their skin to absorb more heat from the sun.

Snakes have very poor eyesight and hearing. They can feel some movement through the ground, but their primary sense is smell. All snakes have nostrils, but the main way they smell is by catching odor molecules with their tongues and passing them back to something called a Jacobson's organ in the top of their mouths. (Lizards and other reptiles and amphibians have Jacobson's organs as well, but for a snake, since it sees so poorly, the Jacobson's organ is much more important.)

A few snakes have an additional sense organ, something that no other animals have. These snakes have special pits on their heads that enable them to detect even very small heat differences from a distance. At night, say, when a mouse goes by, such a snake can sense the mouse's body heat and tell exactly where that heat is coming from. Based on its sense of heat, then, it will strike and kill the mouse!

There are only two poisonous lizards in the world, the Gila monster of the Southwestern United States and the beaded lizard of Mexico. By contrast, hundreds of snakes are poisonous; almost 300 different snakes have strong enough poison that they can kill a man.

The king snake is a constrictor. Rather than using poison to kill its prey, the king snake squeezes them so tightly that they cannot breathe. King snakes prefer to eat other snakes.

Snakes are meat eaters. Though many lizards are meat eaters, others eat plants or insects. One – the marine iguana – eats algae!

Snakes and lizards have at least one feature in common: their skin grows in a single scaly sheet and the scales overlap each other.

The smallest lizards are only a few inches long; the biggest lizard, called the Komodo dragon, lives in India and grows up to nine or ten feet long and can weigh almost 300 pounds. The smallest snake may grow to six inches in length; the largest, as we have said, can be thirty feet long.

Most lizards stay on land, but a few can swim. The lizard called a flying dragon has skin flaps, similar to the skin flaps of flying squirrels and some of the other animals we have studied. Unlike these other animals, the flying dragon's skin flaps are attached to its ribs, so it is actually able to spread its "wings" without jumping from a tree. As with the flying mammals, the flying dragon is able to use these flaps to jump and glide through the air from tree to tree.

Order: Turtles

When you think of a turtle, you may think of the story about the tortoise and the hare. The hare was fast; the tortoise, slow. The hare could have won the race easily if only he would have kept running. The only way the tortoise won was by plodding forward without stopping.

Most turtles are slow, but sea turtles can swim up to twenty miles per hour. And there is a fresh-water turtle in North America that can actually outrun all but the fastest human sprinters.

The loggerhead turtle rarely exceeds 300 pounds today, but it wasn't so long ago, judging by the size of their shells, some loggerhead must have weighed a thousand pounds. Their shells would serve as small rowboats.

The turtle is the one reptile that carries its house on its back. Actually, it's almost unfair to say it carries its shell on its back, because its shell is really partly made from its back bone. The inner layer of the top of the shell is made from the turtle's vertebrae; the inner layer of the bottom of the shell is made from the turtle's ribs. Most turtles have another unique feature besides carrying their house with them. God put their hip and shoulder bones inside their ribs. This means that, when they are attacked, they can draw their heads, legs and tails inside their shells for protection.

Turtles' feet come in three main shapes. Most land turtles have short, stubby feet that look like the end of a club. Fresh water turtles usually have webbed feet—good for walking on land or swimming in water. Sea turtles have legs and feet that look like flippers—kind of like the cetaceans, pinnipeds and sea cows.

Turtles have no teeth. Instead, they have beaks, like birds. They use their beaks to tear their food.

Turtles are some of the longest living animals on earth. Some have been known to live for more than a hundred years. Turtles' skin is like the skin of the crocodilians: it grows not in scales but in larger patches called plates.

Turtles are all oviparous.

There are about 250 species of turtles.

Order: Tuatara

The tuatara (too-uh-TAR-uh) grows to about two feet long and has a series of upright white scales that run down the middle of its back. It looks very much like a large lizard or a very small dinosaur (see the picture of the marine iguana, pg. 130, for a good idea of what a tuatara looks like). Tuataras are like salamanders and lizards in their ability to shed their tails and regrow new ones. They live on a few islands off the coast of New Zealand. The oldest tuatara on record lived seventy-seven years. There is only one species of tuatara.

Vocabulary

viviparous—born live from inside the mother

ovoviviparous—hatched from an egg *inside* the mother, then born

Questions

1. How could you tell the difference between a lizard and a salamander? *(A lizard, being a reptile, has scaly, dry skin; a salamander, being an amphibian, has mucus-wet skin; also, a salamander goes through metamorphosis while a lizard does not.)*
2. How can you distinguish an alligator from a crocodile? *(You can see the large teeth in the bottom jaw of a crocodile even when he closes his mouth; an alligator is able to hide his teeth when he closes his mouth.)*
3. What are some of the differences between lizards and snakes? *(Most lizards have four legs; snakes have none; lizards have eyelids; snakes have none; lizards have ear openings on the outsides of their heads; snakes have none; lizards generally have far fewer vertebrae than the snakes do; Lizards' tails are usually at least as long as their bodies while snakes' tails are only a fraction as long as their bodies.)*
4. There are water snakes and there are land snakes. Caecilians (see page 125) look exactly like small snakes. They tend to live their entire lives either underground or in water. So why do you think scientists say that caecilians are not snakes? What differences must there be between caecilians and snakes? *(Just like the differences between salamanders and lizards, caecilians have mucus-wet skin, lizards have dry, scaly skin; caecilians go through metamorphosis, lizards do not.)*
5. What is a Jacobson's organ and what does it do? *(It is a smell sensor located in the top of amphibians' and reptiles' mouths.)*

6. Why is the Jacobson's organ especially important to snakes? *(because they don't see very well)*
7. What special organs do a few snakes have that no other animal have? *(Special heat-sensing pits on their heads that enable them to detect even very small heat differences from a distance.)*
8. What feature do all lizards and snakes have in common? *(They grow their skin in a single scaly sheet.)*
9. What parts of a turtle's body form its shell? *(Its vertebrae for the top of the shell; its ribs form the lower shell.)*
10. What unique design feature permits many turtles to withdraw their legs inside their shells? *(Their hip and shoulder bones are <u>inside</u> their ribs.)*
11. What are the foot types of the three main types of turtle? *(club foot – land, web foot – fresh water, flipper foot – sea)*
12. What do turtles have instead of teeth? *(beaks)*

Superclass: Fishes

Did you know that not all fish spend all their time—or even most of their time—in water? Some fish don't have scales. And a few fish don't even have fins.

So how can you know a fish when you see one?

Common Characteristics of Fish

- A fish is a cold-blooded vertebrate that, though it may spend significant time on land, must spend at least some time in the water and cold spend its entire life in the water if required to do so. Some other key features:
- All fish have gills. They may not necessarily use them, and their gills may be underdeveloped, but all fish have gills. When they are fully developed, gills allow fish to use oxygen that has been dissolved in water. Many eels

look a lot like water snakes; you can tell the difference between an eel and a snake by the fact that eels have gills, snakes don't. (Eels are fish.)

- ✦ Fish have two-chambered hearts (instead of three- or four-chambered hearts like the amphibians, reptiles, birds and mammals).
- ✦ When comparing a fish to a cetacean like a porpoise or a whale, one of the first things you will notice is that the fish's tail fins stand upright, like the rudder of a boat; cetaceans' tails lie sideways.
- ✦ Most fish lay eggs in the water. After the eggs are laid, then the male spreads his sperms over them so the eggs will be fertilized. Though most fish pay no attention to their eggs or the babies (called "fry"), a few species make nests, watch over them and care for them until they hatch. Usually it is the father who does all these things, though in a few species the mother will do this instead of the father. Very rarely both parents will cooperate in caring for the young.
- ✦ Different fish have different strengths when it comes to their senses. Some fish can see very well. Others are more taste- or smell-oriented. The striped bass has a tremendous ability to feel movements underwater from a distance away. Some fish have taste buds all over their bodies. Some can even "taste" food with their tails!
- ✦ There are three main classes of fish.

Class: Agnatha (Jawless Fish)

The sea lamprey, a jawless fish, gets its nourishment by attaching itself to a fish, rasping a hole in its side, then sucking out the fish's blood and other body fluids.

Most fish have jaws, but a few don't. They have a sucker-disk instead. Jawless fish are mostly known from fossils—only two orders are now living: the lampreys and the hagfish. All told, there are about 45 species in these two orders.

Class: Gnathostomata (Jawed Fish)

The jawed fish include the other two classes: the bony fish and the cartilagenous (car-til-A-jeh-nus; the "A" is pronounced like the a in cat) fish.

Cartilagenous fish have no bones. Instead, their skeletons are made of the bone-like material called cartilage. The piece that runs down the center of your nose and that makes your nose stick out of your face is cartilage. Perhaps you have eaten meat and come across a part you could not chew. The hard piece in the middle of the meat is cartilage. Cartilage is hard but flexible. The cartilagenous fish include sharks, chimaeras (ki-MIR-uhs) and rays.

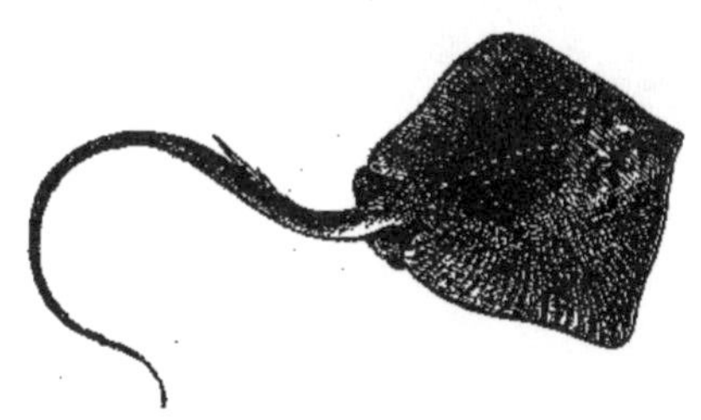

Sting rays are found around the world in warm seas and tropical rivers. An Australian sting ray grows to 750 pounds. If attacked, the sting ray drives one of the spines in the middle of its tail into the flesh of its attacker. It then injects poison which can cause severe pain or even death.

The hammerhead shark has its eyes and nostrils located in the two long side pieces of its skull. Hammerheads grow up to thirteen feet in length and have been known to attack humans.

Bony fish include all the "normal" fish you're aware of, plus eels (which look like snakes) and several fish that look strange enough that you'd think they belong in a Dr. Seuss book.

Some of the more interesting fish include the following:

The Mudskippers

These fish, found in mudflats and swamps from West Africa, across southern Asia to the South Pacific, look as if they are half fish and half frog. They have large gill chambers in which they can store water while they hop about on land.

The Lungfish

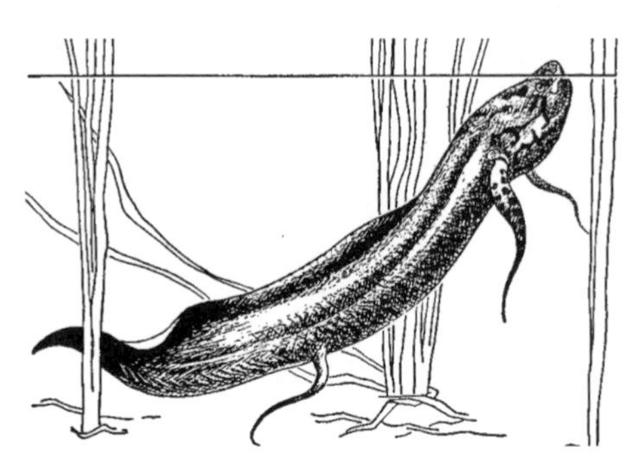

. . . has a large air bladder which it uses as a lung. This is one of those rare fish that has such poorly developed gills, it must breathe air. If it cannot get to the surface of the water, it will drown! Some lungfish have been known to hybernate in blocks of hardened mud for more than four years. Once the mud was softened again, the lungfish took up living where it left off!

The Walking Catfish

. . . can spend days out of water. It has been known to use its side fins and tail to crawl from one lake to another!

The Whale Shark

. . . is the biggest fish in the world. It weighs more than twice as much as an African elephant—close to 30,000 pounds!

The Electric Eel

... uses special muscles to put out electrical charges of up to 650 volts. These charges often kill, but always at least stun, the eel's prey (and its enemies!). Since the eel has no teeth or any other way to defend itself, one can see its electrical capabilities are very important.

The Flounder

... begins life looking pretty much like any ordinary fish, but then, once it is about half an inch long, one of its eyes moves over to the other side of its head so that the two eyes are next to each other on that one side. About the same time, the flounder acquires the ability to change colors with its environment. Once this happens, the flounder can lie on the bottom of the ocean, looking just like the rocks, pebbles, or whatever that surround it, yet be in a good position to catch any other fish that happen to wander by. The bottom of a flounder (when it is lying on the bottom of the ocean) is white; the top side will look almost exactly like whatever it is laying on.

The Black-Chinned Mouthbreeder

... hatches its eggs in its mouth! After scooping out a nest in the bottom muck, the mother lays her eggs and the father immediately picks them up in his mouth. In fact, if he doesn't pick them up fast enough, the mother will batter him with her tail! It takes a week or two for the fry to hatch, and during that time, the father eats nothing!

THE COELACANTHS (SEE-LUH-KANTHS)

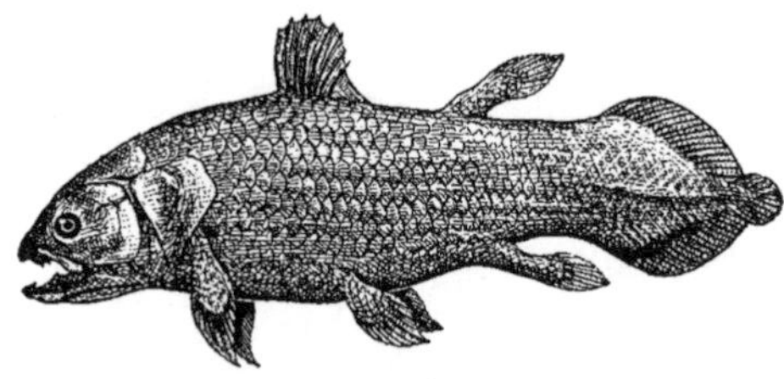

. . . are a group of fish that most zoologists thought had been ***extinct*** for sixty million years or more, until 1938, when a fishing boat off the coast of South Africa caught a nearly five-foot sample. Since then, several others have also been caught.

THE ATLANTIC MACKEREL

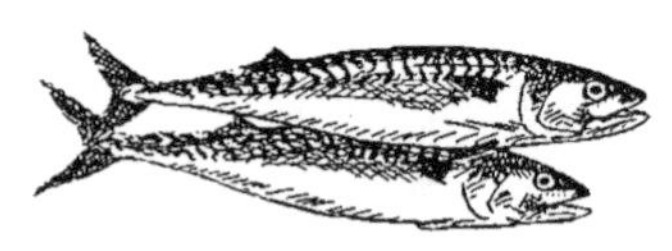

. . . can never rest. Its gills are less efficient than other fish's, so if it stops swimming, it will suffocate. By swimming around, it forces fresh water—and oxygen—through its gills and into its bloodstream.

THE PIRANHA

Many people have heard the myth that the piranha is the world's deadliest fish. Piranhas do have sharp teeth, and they will eat a dead animal or person they find in the water in almost no time at all. But they are timid animals, and will not attack living humans. They prefer to nip the end of another fish's tail than to try to eat the whole fish.

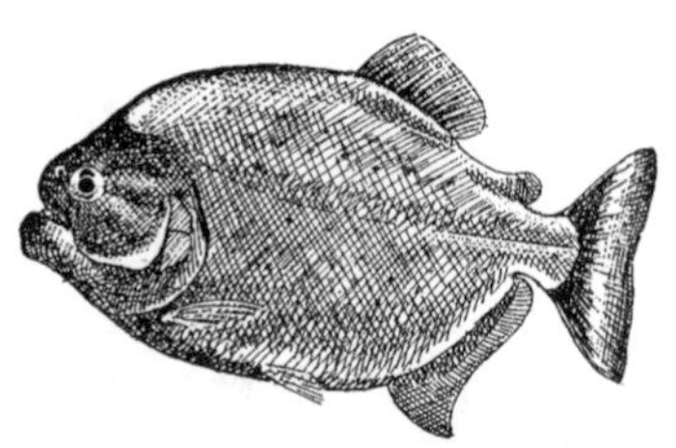

People who live near piranhas in South America understand them, but when tourists come and see them tearing apart a dead animal, they are amazed and the myth grows. Teddy Roosevelt once wrote, "They will snap a finger off a hand incautiously trailed in the water. They will rend and devour alive any wounded man or beast." Because of his letter and accounts from other visitors, the legend of the piranha still lives strong today.[14]

The Fourspine Stickleback

. . . builds a nest in which to hatch its eggs, just like a bird. Here, a father stickleback weaves some plants together to form the nest. Once his wife lays eggs in the nest, he will weave a roof . . . then leave to find another wife!

The Seahorse

. . . has a head that looks like a horse, a prehensile tail like New World monkeys, the body of a tiny dragon, and a pouch like most marsupials!

When a mother seahorse lays her eggs, the father picks them up and puts them in a pouch at the bottom of his belly where he carries them around until they hatch.

Because the seahorse has only a dorsal (back) fin, it is usually pushed about by the sea currents. By using its tail to grab onto seaweed, it is able to give itself a little more control over its life!

---

[14] To find out more, read "Relax, It's Only a Piranha" in the July, 1999 publication of *Smithsonian Magazine*. You can read this article online at http://www.smithsonianmag.si.edu/.

Vocabulary

dorsal – back

extinct – having died out, no longer in existence

prehensile – grasping

fry – baby fish

Questions

1. What is the biggest fish in the world and how much does it weigh? *(The whale shark; it weighs up to 30,000 pounds!)*
2. How do jawless fish eat? *(They use their sucker disks to attach themselves to a source of food, and then suck it in.)*
3. Think of the way the sea lamprey eats: it gets its food from other fish. There was a special word we used when we talked about plants that get their nourishment from other plants. The same word can be applied to the lamprey. What is the word? *(parasite)*
4. How would you be able to tell the difference between a fish that can spend lots of time on land and an amphibian (that can spend lots of time in water)? *(The fish doesn't go through metamorphosis.)*
5. Name at least three differences between fish (like sharks) and cetaceans (like porpoises and whales). *(Fish have upright tail fins; cetaceans have horizontal tail fins; fish are cold-blooded, cetaceans are warm-blooded; cetaceans have mammary glands, fish do not.)*

Questions About Vertebrates

1. What are two distinguishing characteristics of each of the five classes?
2. What are the five major classes of vertebrates? *(fishes, amphibians, reptiles, birds, and mammals)*

INVERTEBRATES

Did you think we were done talking about animals? We haven't talked about even half of the different types of animals in the world!

Of course the animals we have mentioned so far include all the big animals. But the big animals, the vertebrates, include only about 40,000 different species. The invertebrates—all the rest of the animals—include many more than a million species!

Can you think of some animals that don't have backbones?

How about all the insects? (They make up the majority of the invertebrates—more than a million species on their own.)

Then there are the shellfish: clams, oysters, and octopuses.

And snails.

Slugs. Centipedes. Worms. Jellyfish. Sponges.

Sponges?

Yes. Sponges are animals.

Even though there are more invertebrates than vertebrates, we won't spend as much time on them as we have on the vertebrate animals. But we should at least get to know them a little.

Phylum: Porifera (Sponges)

Most of the cleaning instruments we call sponges are made by people from rubber or plastic. But until fifty years ago or so, all sponges came from the ocean. The sponges we get from the ocean are actually the skeletons of animals called sponges.

Sponges make up their own phylum, Porifera. Porifera means "having pores." A **pore**, as we have already noted, is a small hole.

Sponges come in all kinds of wonderful shapes and sizes. Some sponges grow to less than an inch in diameter and some to more than four feet. Some look like giant eggs, others like short, fat worms. Some look like beautiful plants, others like fungi. If you didn't know better, you'd never think a sponge was an animal. Some sponges are bright orange, or yellow, purple, brown or grey. Some are sparkling pink and blue.

Sponges live in water. Most live in the ocean, but a few can be found in lakes, rivers and streams.

Sponges reproduce either simply by growing from a piece of another sponge, or by growing from a single cell inside a "parent" sponge. A cell that will grow into a new sponge first floats around in the water. At this point it is called a larva (LAR-va). Many other kinds of invertebrates have young that are also called larvae. When a sponge larva reaches the right size, it finds a place it wants for its home. Then it attaches itself to that spot. It will stay there for the rest of its life. As it grows into an adult, it forms into one of the shapes described above.

Sponges take minerals from the water around them to build shells or skeletons for their bodies. Scientists classify sponges according to what they use to make their skeletons. Some sponges use a mineral called calcium carbonate (that's the same thing limestone and chalk are made of). Some sponges use silica (the stuff of sand and glass). Some use silica and a kind of rubbery material called spongin (SPUN-jin). When we talk about natural sponges for use in washing, it is only this last type of sponge, the type that has a spongin skeleton, that we will use.

All sponges are hollow. Not only are they hollow; they are also porous (having lots of pores). In addition to being hollow and porous, they have one large hole at one end. This large hole is called the **osculum** (OSS-cue-lum). Sponges pull water in through their pores and then push it out through their osculums.

Sponges don't have mouths and stomachs like we do, but many of the cells that line their bodies can absorb any food that washes by.

Phylum: Coelenterates (sill-EN-ter-its)

The coelenterates include all the jellyfish, sea anemones (uh-NEH-moh-nees), and corals as well as some small animals called hydras. Some coelenterates are only a quarter of an inch across; the arctic jellyfish can grow to seven feet in diameter!

There are about 9,000 different species of coelenterates.

The word coelenterate means "having a hollow intestine." Coelenterates' bodies are hollow, just like sponges'. Unlike sponges, however, coelenterates don't have pores; they have one opening into their insides. They bring food in through this opening, and the part of the food that they cannot use leaves through this opening as well. Most coelenterates have **tentacles**—long, dangly fingers—that surround the opening. They use these tentacles to grab their food. Many coelenterates have special stinging cells in their tentacles which they use to paralyze their prey.

Instead of living by themselves, many coelenterates live together in colonies. Coral is a good example. Each tiny hole in a piece of coral is like an "apartment house" for a coral animal to live in. The members of a coral colony all cooperate with one another to get food.

Coelenterates have several different ways of reproducing. Some sea anemones just pinch in half to become two animals instead of one! Many coelenterates produce eggs and sperms, which must join together in the same way that the pollen and ovule in a plant must join together, to produce a larva. And some coelenterates produce eggs and sperms, which join to become larvae, which grow into baby anemones, which then break apart to become jellyfish!

Vocabulary

pore—small hole

osculum—the large hole at one end of a sponge

tentacle—a long, dangly, finger-like organ

Questions

1. What are the different materials that sponges use to make their skeletons? *(Calcium carbonate – the same material from which limestone and chalk are made of; silica – the same material as sand is made from; and spongin – a kind of rubbery substance.)*
2. Would it be okay to say that the osculumis a sponge's mouth? Why or why not? *(No, because sponges take food <u>in</u> through their pores and they excrete their wastes through their osculums.)*
3. How do sponges reproduce? *(Either by growing new sponges from pieces that break off of old ones, or by growing from single cells inside of older sponges.)*
4. What does the word coelenterate mean? *(having a hollow-intestine)*
5. How do coelenterates reproduce? *(By splitting in half, through sexual reproduction, using eggs and sperms, or by sexual reproduction and then splitting in half!)*

Worms

There are many different kinds of worms. Zoologists don't agree on how to arrange them into groups. We will look at the three major phyla.

Phylum: Nematodes (NEE-muh-todes; Roundworms)

The nematodes or roundworms are parasites; most of them live in and get their food from other animals. Some roundworms, however, live on their own in water, dirt, or dead plants and animals.

Most roundworms are oviparous. As we learned before, that means they lay and are born from eggs. One species of roundworm lays almost 200,000 eggs a day for ten months in a row!

As you can imagine, especially when they lay that many eggs, there are a lot of roundworms in the world. One group of scientists counted the number of roundwoms they could find in a rotten apple. They counted more than 90,000 of them! There are about 10,000 different species of roundworms. They range in size from being so small you need a microscope to see them to being three feet long.

Some of the more common varieties of roundworm include the hair snake or hairworm which can grow to two feet or more in length, and the hookworm which is a common parasite in the southern United States. People who lived on farms used to find hairworms wriggling about in the horses' water trough. The reason they were called hairworms is because they looked like a long hair—maybe like a hair from a horse's tail.

Roundworms cause a lot of illness among people around the world. Sometimes they make people sick with awful diarrhea or pneumonia. But they kill people, too. (A lot of children die from diarrhea.)

Phylum: Flatworms

There are somewhere between 6,500 and 7,000 different flatworms in the world. Like the roundworms, some of these live on their own; others are parasites. Flatworms, like their name implies, are slightly flattened. They have a true top, bottom, left and right sides. Most flatworms are too small to see and cause few problems to human beings.

Tapeworms are a special type of flatworm and they cause real problems.

Tapeworms grow in vertebrate animals' intestines or in their muscles. Doctors have found tapeworms as long as thirty feet living inside of people. As you can imagine, if you have a few big tapeworms living inside you, eating all your food, you might have a hard time getting enough food for yourself! The most likely way for you to get tapeworms is by eating meat that hasn't been cooked well enough.

Phylum: Annelids (ANN-uh-lids; Segmented ["Ring"] Worms)

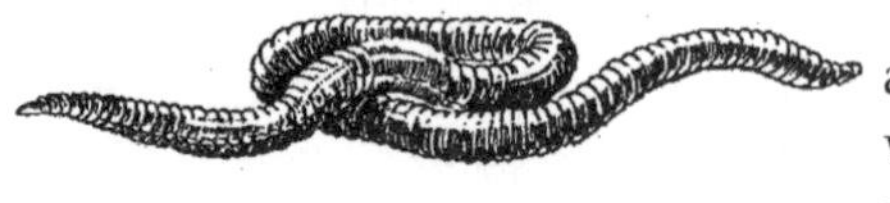

The third type of worms are called annelids. The word annelid means "ringed worm." These are the "true" worms, the earthworms you find on the sidewalk after a rainstorm, and the kinds of worms fishermen stick on their hooks to catch fish.

Annelids' bodies are segmented; each segment looks a little like a ring (or a car tire). Ringed worms live on land (I should say, under land!) and in water. All of them have segments. They also have a head and a digestive tract. Some annelids have legs. If a ringed worm has legs, its legs are unjointed and don't bend.

Scientists have identified about seven thousand species of ringed worms!

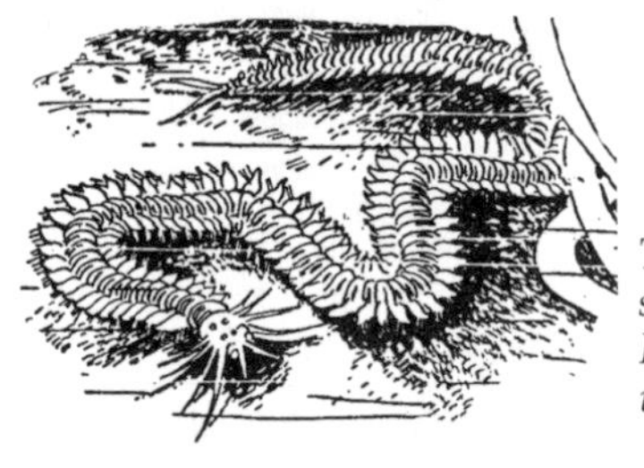

*The sand worm is an **annelid** that lives in the sand in tidepools along the Atlantic and Pacific coasts of the United States. Notice its unjointed legs.*

Phylum: Echinoderms (ee-KINE-oh-derms)

Sea urchins, sand dollars, starfish, and sea cucumbers are all echinoderms.

Echinoderm means "spiny skinned." Echinoderms have spiny skin. They are sea animals. The spines that stick out of their skin are parts of their skeletons. The rest of their skeletons, however, are inside their bodies.

Echinoderms have radial symmetry (see page 66). Their bodies are laid out in a circular pattern, like the petals on a flower or like a tube. In the center of the tube, you will find the echinoderm's mouth.

Stretching away from the mouth are five sections.[1]

Echinoderms are the only animals that have suction cups called **tube feet**. These tube feet are arranged in rows that extend from their mouths out to the edges of the echinoderms' bodies. Underneath the tube feet there are small canals. Echinoderms use their tube feet to guide food down these canals to their mouths. A starfish will use its suction power to grab a clam or oyster and force its shell open. The starfish will then push its stomach outside its body, between the halves of the clam or oyster shell, and digest the clam or oyster right on the spot!

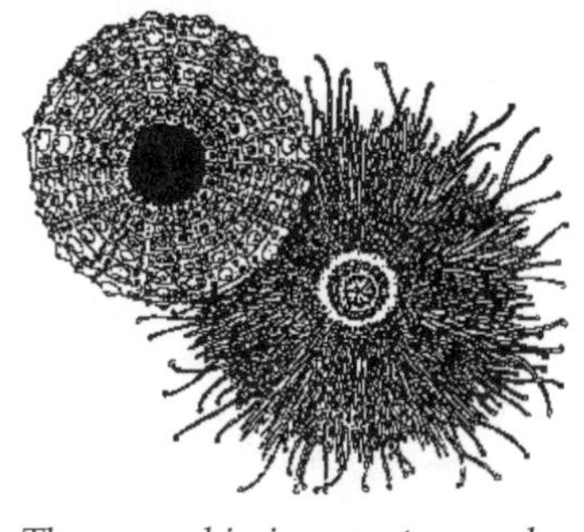

The sea urchin is a great example of the spiny-skinned echinoderms! Above is both a living sea urchin (lower right) and a "test," which is a limestone shell the sea urchin has to protect its body. Notice that, even though the sea urchin as a whole simply looks round, the test is divided, as all echinoderms are, into five sections. In this case, each section includes one wide ring and one narrow ring.

Starfish have that amazing ability we noticed that some salamanders and lizards have: if they think they need to, they can release one of their arms and grow a new one in its place. In fact, if a starfish is chopped in half, it can

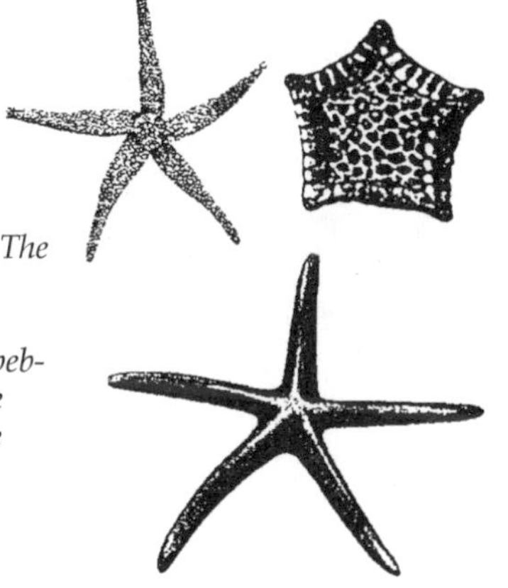

Starfish come in a number of shapes and sizes. The Linckia laevigata (bottom) is almost 15 inches across and has a relatively smooth surface; the Nardoa pauciforis (upper left), however, has a pebbly surface and is only seven inches across. The Ceramaster placenta (upper right) has the same five-pointed appearance, but is only five inches across and looks like it is made of snakeskin.

---

[1]Some starfish have more than five sections. One species found along the California coast has 6, another Pacific variety, the Sun Star, has 23, and some species have up to forty arms!

often grow a complete new starfish from any piece that has a part of the central disk! Some scientists are trying to figure out how and why starfish can do these things. They hope to use whatever they learn to help people regrow arms or legs if they are chopped off!

In order to have babies, starfish, sea urchins, and other echinoderms produce millions of eggs and sperms. Like many invertebrates, each individual echinoderm is both a mother and a father! It makes both eggs and sperms! These eggs and sperms are then released into the ocean. There must be millions of them in order for an egg and sperm to find each other, join together, and grow into a larva! Echinoderm larvae float around near the surface of the ocean until they get big enough to settle down to the bottom and turn into adults.

Phylum: Mollusks

The mollusks are divided into six major classes. Three are familiar: **Gastropods** ("stomach-foots") include the slugs and snails; Pelecypods (pell-EH-si-pods; "winged-foots") are all the two-shelled (or "bivalve") creatures like clams, scallops and oysters; and **Cephalopods** (SEH-feh-low-pods; "head-foots") include the squids and octopuses.

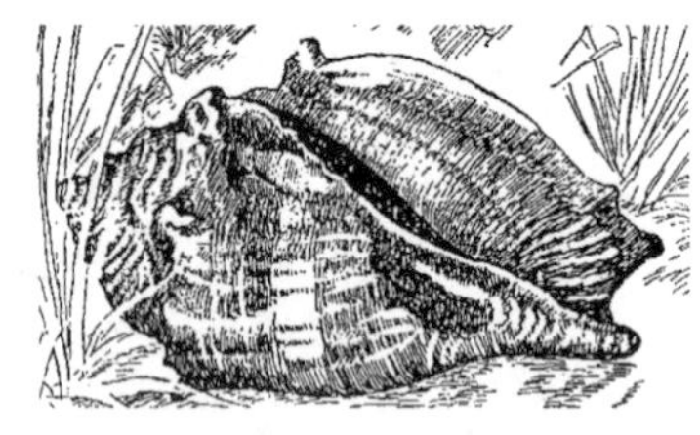

The conch is a large, snail-like animal with a heavy, spiny shell that is usually beautifully colored in pinks and oranges.

Mollusks can be found in the highest mountains, the deepest oceans, and in freshwater lakes and streams. The greatest number of varieties live in the sea. There are so many varieties—around 80,000 species, almost twice as many as all the vertebrates put together—that you've probably seen some.

Mollusks are soft-bodied animals, with no skeleton (although many have shells). Their skin could be described as similar to amphibians' in that it is always moist. They, too, use mucus to keep damp.

Slugs are basically snails without shells. They have the same body parts, including a special foot they use to creep along. Slugs and snails—the gastropods—have teeth on their tongues, which they use to scrape food into their mouths. Some gastropods are vegetarians, while others stalk and eat prey. Some ocean-dwelling snails use a deadly poison similar to that of a snake!

The **bivalves** or two-shelled mollusks (bi- means two, valves are shells) all live in the water. Some bivalves, such as clams, may dig in the sand with their foot; others, such as mussels, attach themselves to rocks with special threads. Because they cannot move around very well (or at all!) bivalves must wait for their food to come to them, just as the sponges do. As they pump water through their bodies, they filter out tiny plants and animals for food. They also filter out the oxygen they need to breathe.

The "feet" of squids and octopuses are divided into "arms": octopuses have eight arms (octo- means eight) while squids have ten.

Although many people think octopuses are dangerous and aggressive, they really are very timid. They would rather hide or run away than fight. Octopuses can change their skin coloring to blend in with their surroundings. They may squirt a dark ink into the water, and jet away to escape while a confused predator tries to eat the "ink octopus." When they are cornered, octopuses are capable of biting with their sharp beaks (located where their arms meet). Some octopuses are poisonous as well.

Octopuses are among the most intelligent of all invertebrates.

Vocabulary

tube feet—suction cup feet; only echinoderms have them

gastropod—stomach foot

cephalopod—head-foot

bivalve—having two shells

Questions

1. What are the three main phylums of worms? *(nematodes, roundworms, flatworms, and annelids [segmented worms])*
2. What phylum of worms seems to cause the most problems for humans, and why? *(The nematodes; because they are parasites.)*
3. How many eggs can one species of roundworm lay each day? *(200,000!)*
4. How many roundworms did some scientists count in a single rotten apple? *(90,000!)*
5. Why do ringed worms have the name they do? *(because their segments look like rings)*
6. What is special about the legs of ringed worms that have legs? *(they are unjointed; they cannot bend)*
7. Why do scientists say worms are different from snakes? *(worms have no backbones, snakes do)*
8. What does echinoderm mean? *(spiny-skinned)*
9. How are echinoderms similar to some flowers? *(they have radial symmetry)*
10. Most echinoderms have how many sections? *(five)*
11. What strange thing will a starfish do in order to eat a clam or oyster? *(It will push its stomach outside of its body to digest the clam or oyster out there.)*
12. What special ability do starfish have similar to only a few other animals? *(They can regrow severed body parts.)*
13. Where do echinoderm larvae live? *(at the surface of the ocean)*

14. What sets mollusks apart from other animals? *(They have soft bodies and have no skeleton.)*

15. Mollusks have "skin very similar to amphibians'." Why, then, aren't mollusks amphibians? *(Among other reasons: because they are invertebrates; amphibians are vertebrates.)*

16. Where will you find a gastropod's teeth? *(on its tongue)*

17. Octopuses can do something that only a very few other animals can do. What is that? *(They can change color to match their environment.)*

18. What defensive strategies will an octopus use besides changing its color? *(It will squirt a cloud of ink to confuse its enemy, then swim quickly away; if it needs to, it will bite with its beak; some octopuses also have poison.)*

Phylum: Arthropods

The word arthropod means "jointed foot." The arthropods include all the invertebrates that have jointed legs: all the lobsters, barnacles, spiders, scorpions, and insects . . . as well as thousands of others.

The arthropods alone make up more than a million species, and scientists are finding and naming some ten to twenty thousand new species every year!

Besides having jointed legs, there are a few other things to know about arthropods.

Arthropods have no internal skeletons. Instead, their body walls are made of a tough material called chitin (KITE-n). Scientists say these animals have an exoskeleton. Exo- means "outside." Arthropods' skeletons are on the outside of their bodies.

Besides having exoskeletons, arthropods also have a very simple blood circulation system. Rather than a piped circulation system like the circulation systems of mammals and birds,[2]

---

[2]Veins and arteries act like pipes!

arthropods' circulation systems are more like a bathtub filled with water in which a squeeze bottle is repeatedly filled with water and squeezed. If the bottle is repeatedly squeezed and filled, and if it always points in the same direction, pretty soon the water in the bathtub will begin to move around in a circle—circulate. That's the way arthropods' circulation systems work. Their hearts are just like open-topped squeeze bottles. An arthropod's heart is in the back end of its body and the heart's open end points toward the front of the arthropod's body.

You may be surprised to learn that arthropods have blood. If you have ever squished a bug, you realize that their blood, if they have any, isn't red.

Our blood has iron in it, which is why it is red. But instead of iron, arthropods have copper in their blood, which gives it a green color!

Let's take a quick look at just a few of the more important classes of arthropods.

Class: Crustaceans

Crustaceans have two pairs of antennas (four antennas, total) and at least five pairs of legs. They also have a crust (that's where they get their name) that covers and holds together their head and thorax (chest). Most crustaceans breathe by means of gills. The smallest crustacean is the water flea which isn't even a hundredth of an inch long. The Japanese crab, on the other hand, stretches ten feet!

Crustaceans include, among other animals, all the crabs, lobsters, barnacles, shrimps, and crayfish or crawdaddies.

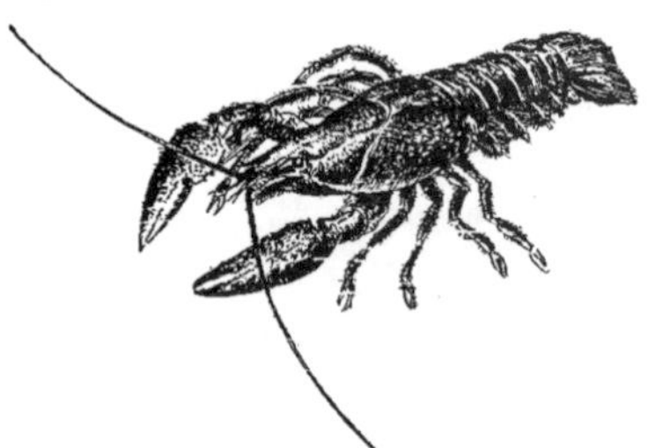

The crayfish or crawdaddy looks like a miniature lobster. They prefer fresh water and can be found throughout the United States living under rocks in streams, rivers, and ponds. Others prefer to burrow in the mud in swamps and marshes.

Class: Centipedes (Chilopods) and Millipedes (Diplopods)

The name centipede means "hundred foot." Chilopod, the scientific name for centipedes, means exactly the same thing: "hundred foot." Millipede means "thousand foot." But the scientific name for millipedes, diplopod, means "two foot"!

Centipedes and millipedes both have segmented bodies and in this way they are like ringed worms. However, they both also have jointed legs which sets them apart from the ringed worms. Notice that the millipede (below) has two pairs of legs per segment, while the centipede (above) has only one. The house centipede we are likely to find in our houses (above) has only thirty legs.

Why? Why would one have the same scientific name and common name, and the other have a scientific name that means something completely different from its common name?

Once you understand the difference between millipedes and centipedes, you'll know why.

Both centipedes and millipedes have lots and lots of legs. Centipedes can have up to 340 legs. Millipedes, however, never have more than 230 legs. That's pretty amazing since their name says they have a thousand legs!

I don't know why the name of the animal with fewer legs says it has more, but I can tell you why the millipede has that strange scientific name diplopod.

Both centipedes and millipedes have segmented bodies. In this way, they are just alike the segmented worms. They differ from worms, however, in that their legs are jointed. Further, centipedes are different from millipedes because centipedes have one pair of legs per segment while millipedes have two. In other words, millipedes have four legs coming out of each of the segments of their bodies. Maybe that's why they are called millipedes even though they don't have a thousand legs: they look like they have more legs because their legs are more jammed together than the legs of centipedes.

Millipedes eat decaying plants; centipedes prefer eating insects and spiders. They kill their prey with poison. Centipede bites can be very painful to people but they normally won't kill a person.

Class: Arachnids

Arachnids are arthropods with four pairs of legs. Spiders are arachnids. So are scorpions, ticks and mites.

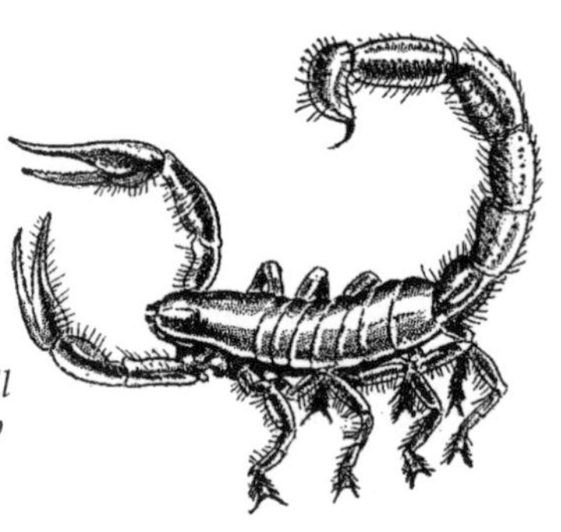

Scorpions (right) are night hunters who enjoy eating spiders and insects. They kill their prey with the poison sting at the tip of their tails.

The black widow spider is poisonous but, because it is usually small, its bite is rarely fatal. The spider can be recognized by a bright red, hourglass marking on the bottom of its abdomen (left). The black widow gets its name from the females' habit of eating their husbands. This practice is not unique to black widows; other spiders do the same.

Vocabulary

exoskeleton—a skeleton on the *outside* of the body

chitin—the tough material of which arthropods' exoskeletons are made

thorax—chest

Questions

1. What does the word arthropod mean? *(jointed leg)*
2. Besides having jointed legs, what else sets arthropods apart from other animals? *(They have exoskeletons, they have a "bathtub"-like circulation system, and their blood has copper in it instead of iron.)*
3. What color is arthropod blood? *(green)*
4. What sets crustaceans apart from other animals? *(They have two pairs of antennas [four antennas, total] and at least five pairs of legs [ten total]; they also have a crust that covers and holds together their head and thorax; most crustaceans breathe by means of gills – which means they live in water.)*
5. What does the word centipede mean? *(hundred foot)* And chilopod? *(also, hundred foot)* And millipede? *(thousand foot)* How about diplopod? *(two foot)*
6. Why would scientists ever call a creature that has dozens and sometimes hundreds of legs a diplopod? *(because it has two pairs of legs per segment of its body)*
7. Which has more legs: a millipede or a centipede? *(a centipede)*
8. If it has fewer legs than a centipede ("hundred foot"), why would people call a millipede a millipede ("thousand foot")? *(Because, with its two pairs of legs per segment, it looks like it may have more legs.)*
9. Do millipedes and centipedes have different eating habits? If so, how do they differ? *(Millipedes eat decaying vegetation; centipedes prefer insects and spiders.)*
10. How can you tell the difference between a centipede and a ringed worm with legs? *(The ringed worm's legs will have no joints; the centipede's legs, by contrast, will have joints.)*
11. What sets arachnids apart from other animals? *(They are arthropods that have four pairs of legs.)*

Class: Insects

The name insect means "cut in." Ants are an excellent example of what this means: their bodies almost look as if they are cut apart: their heads are distinct from their thoraxes (chests), and their thoraxes are distinct from their abdomens.

The problem is, based on this description, spiders seems like they ought to be insects (see the picture of the black widow, above), and many insects—beetles, for instance—don't seem to fit.

But there is another and perhaps easier way to distinguish an insect from other arthropods. That is to notice that insects always have three pairs of legs (six legs, total). Arachnids have eight legs and crustaceans have ten.

Insects also always have one—and only one—pair of antennas. As we noted before, crustaceans have two pairs of antennas.

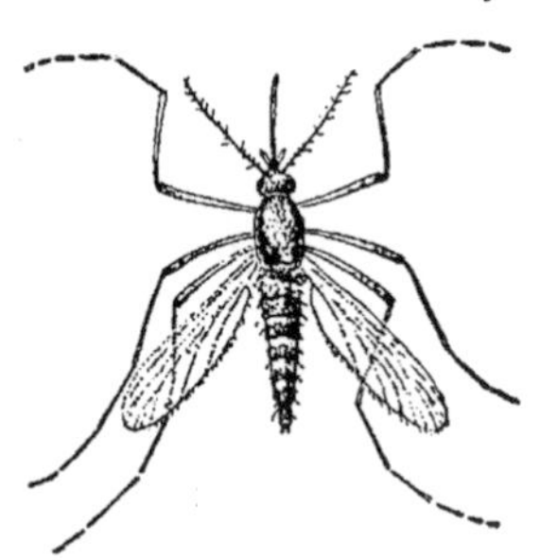

The swamp mosquito is a typical insect with distinct head, thorax and abdomen, six legs, and two antennas.

We could say more about the way insects are built, but there are probably some more interesting things for us to notice.

Insects are oviparous. From the time they are eggs to the time they are adults, insects go through three or four stages that, together, are called metamorphosis.

In a three-step metamorphosis the insect starts as an egg and hatches as a nymph. A nymph looks more or less like an adult except it usually doesn't have wings. Over time, the nymph will grow to become an adult.

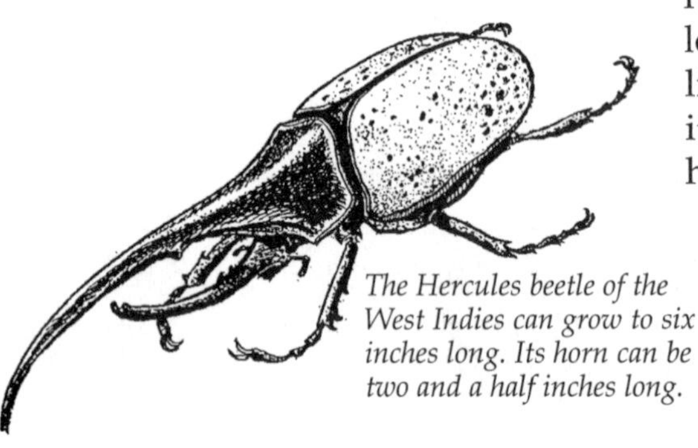

The Hercules beetle of the West Indies can grow to six inches long. Its horn can be two and a half inches long.

The four-step metamorphosis also starts at the egg stage. When four-step insects hatch from their eggs, they are so different from the adults, scientists don't even call them nymphs. They call them larvae. Moth and butterfly larvae are called caterpillars. Fly and beetle larvae are called grubs or, sometimes, worms (though, of course, they aren't real worms).

Robber flies are large, strong, very fast . . . and can even kill wasps and bumblebees as they fly. Robber fly larvae live in rotting wood or vegetation and eat other insect larvae.

As nymphs and larvae grow, they molt—they shed their skins, just like many reptiles do. Each time a nymph or larva molts, it comes out looking a little differently from the way it looked before.

Each species of insect molts a certain number of times. Then it stops. When nymphs stop molting, they are adults. When larvae stop molting, they have to go through one more step. Larvae become what scientists call pupas. Moths and butterflies spin cocoons around their bodies and then become pupas. Other insects allow their skin to dry out and become hard. Scientists call this hard, dry covering a chrysalis. Once this type of insect is inside its chrysalis, then it becomes a pupa.

There is a third type of larvae. These larvae live inside of plants or animals and they simply stay where they are and become pupas.

The May fly spends up to three years of its life as a nymph eating underwater plants before it comes to the surface of the water, molts its skin, and flies to a nearby bush or tree. After one more molt, it is an adult. It lives only a few days more—just long enough to mate and drop eggs in the water.

During the pupa stage, larvae become adults: caterpillars turn into moths or butterflies, and grubs become beetles or flies.

The seventeen-year cicada (sih-CAY-duh) spends even more time as a nymph than does the May fly. It is a nymph for seventeen years!

"Good night. Sleep tight. Don't let the bed bugs bite!" we tell each other when we go to bed. There's a good reason to avoid bed bugs (below right): they get their food by sucking human blood! Improved hygiene has made them less common than they used to be.

Another bothersome pest is the cockroach (below left). Originally from the Orient, they are now found everywhere around the world.

Two final insects: the praying mantis (bottom right) named for its habit of sitting in a position that looks much like prayer and (bottom left) the walking stick, a brown insect designed to look exactly like a twig and thus escape detection.

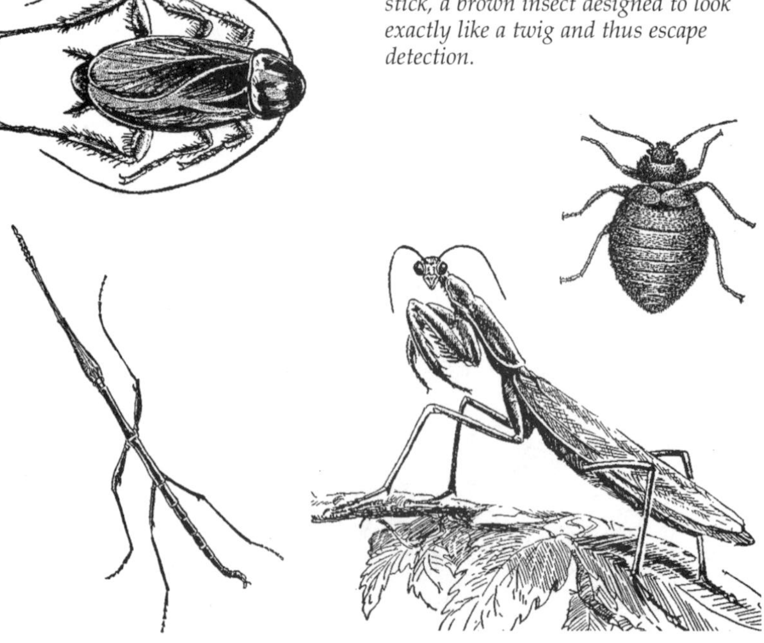

Vocabulary

nymph—a newly hatched three-stage metamorphosis insect

caterpillar—the larva of a moth or butterfly

grub—the larva of a fly or beetle

molt—to shed one's skin

pupa—the final stage before adulthood in a four-stage metamorphosis insect

chrysalis—the hard, dried-out skin of an insect larva that surrounds and protects the insect while it is in the third stage—the pupa stage—of a four-stage metamorphosis

cocoon—the spun fiber sack that surrounds and protects moths and butterflies while they are in the pupa stage of their four-stage metamorphosis

Questions

1. What does the word insect mean? *(cut in)*
2. What differentiates insects from all other animals? *(They are arthropods that have three pairs of legs [six total] and only one pair of antennas.)*
3. Can you name a kind of coelenterate? *(jellyfish, sea anemone, coral, hydra)*
4. What are two of the three kinds of worms? *(round, flat, ringed, or segmented)*
5. Can you name three mollusks? *(slug, snail, clam, oyster, octopus)*
6. What are two types of arthropods other than insects? *(scorpions, spiders, lobsters, crayfish . . .)*
7. What should be a scientist's first clue that a caecilian is not a worm? *(Caecilians have backbones; worms do not.)*

THE PROTISTA (PRO-TEE-STA) KINGDOM

When we first talked about living things, we said that there are two main kingdoms—plants and animals. But not all living things fit into one of these two groups. In addition to the plants and animals we have studied, there is a third kingdom. This kingdom is called the protista (pro-TEE-sta), and members of it are called protists (PRO-teests).[1]

The protists include the **protozoans** (pro-tuh-ZOH-uhns), which are all the one-celled creatures of the world. Scientists have classified more than 30,000 different protozoans. They are very tiny. No one had ever seen a protozoan until Anton van Leeuwenhoek, a Dutch scientist, made his first microscope in the 1670s.

There are other kinds of protists besides the protozoans. The fungi (FUN-jigh) include mushrooms, yeast, and mildew. Algae (AL-jee) such as seaweed and green pond "scum" are also protists. Finally, bacteria are usually grouped in this kingdom as well.

Protozoans

Sometimes when we talk about "germs," what we are really talking about is protozoans. Many diseases are caused by protozoans. For example, the disease called malaria is caused by a single-celled organism called Plasmodium, which can live

[1]Some biologists also divide protists into a fourth or even fifth kingdom.

in human blood. Nowadays we have medicines that can help people not feel so sick when they have malaria, but more than a million people die from malaria each year anyway. Not so long ago, a lot more people died from it.

African sleeping sickness is another fatal disease caused by a protozoan.

As with so many of the other living things, we will only touch on some of the types of protozoans.

The Sarcodines

Sarcodines (SAR-ko-deens or SAR-ko-dines) are one-celled creatures that move about and gather their food by forming **pseudopods** (SUE-doh-pods; false feet; pseudo- means "false"; pod means "foot").

Sarcodines' bodies look a bit like globby goo. They can change shape in almost any way they want. When they want to move in a particular direction, they push out a portion of the wall of their body to form a pseudopod—the "false foot," a portion of their body that sticks out from the rest. They then allow their innards, the **cytoplasm** (see pg. 18), which is rather like jelly, to flow into the pseudopod.

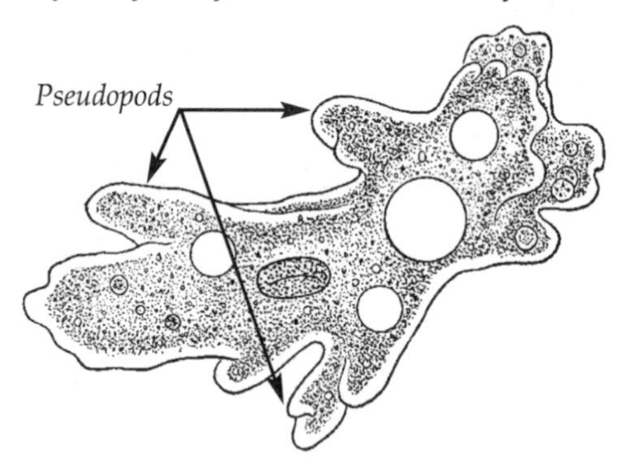

If a sarcodine allows all of its cytoplasm to fill the pseudopod, what happens? The rest of its body comes along! If a sarcodine only partially fills its pseudopod, it can use the pseudopod like an arm or a leg—to move other things (things other than itself) around.

Amoebas (uh-MEE-buhs) are a kind of sarcodine. Amoebas can be found virtually everywhere around the world. They are in the air, on the land, in the sea. But they are most active near the surface of shallow bodies of water, either salt water or fresh.

As amoebas move along, they seem to absorb whatever is smaller than themselves that is in their path. If they can use what they absorb, they use it; if they absorb something they don't want, they leave it behind as they move on.

Amoebas reproduce by splitting themselves in two. They form two pseudopods that stretch in opposite directions. After they duplicate their genetic information[2] and send one copy to one pseudopod and the other to the other pseudopod, they then split right down the middle. Suddenly there are two small amoebas where one large amoeba used to be!

When an amoeba finds that the water in which it is living is drying up, or if the water becomes so polluted that the amoeba cannot continue to live, it pulls in all its pseudopods so it becomes perfectly round. Then it thickens and hardens its "skin." In a sense, it goes to sleep. It can stay in this inactive state for many months or maybe even years.

If the water surrounding it dries up, a blast of wind may pick it up and carry it to another puddle or pond. If it thinks the new environment is safe, it will break through its toughened shell and resume its former life just as if nothing had happened.

Foraminifera (FOR-uh-min-IH-fer-uh)

There are close to twelve hundred different species of foraminifera. Foraminifers are very similar to amoebas except for one thing: they build shells around themselves. **Foraminifers** (FOR-uh-MIN-ih-fers) are one-celled creatures (like the amoebas); they have pseudopods; but they live inside shells that they

[2]The design and operational information contained in a cell's nucleus. See page 22.

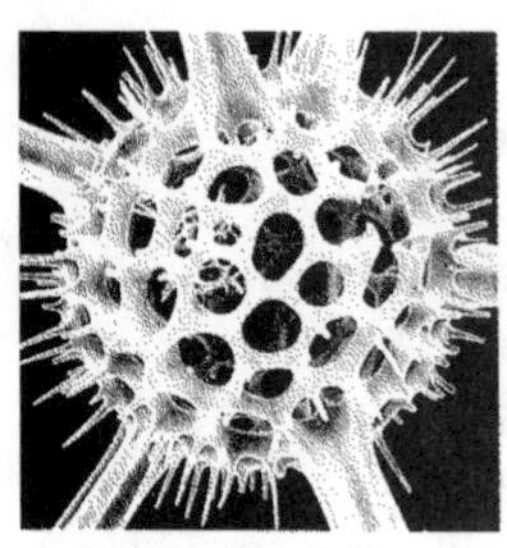

A foraminifer shell. Notice all the foramens where the foraminifer's pseudopods would normally stick out if it were alive.

build. Their shells, made of lime or silica, have many tiny holes in them. These holes are called foramena (foh-RAY-men-uh). The foraminifers are named after their foramena.

Foraminifers stick their pseudopods through these holes. Foraminifers' pseudopods aren't lumpy and broad, like amoebas' pseudopods; they are long and skinny and look almost like tentacles. Some foraminifer pseudopods even branch out so they look like branches with twigs.

Why should we care about the foraminifers? One reason: chalk is made up of millions of foraminifer shells. Limestone is also made of foraminifer shells. The bottom of the ocean is covered with a gray, muddy ooze. That, too, is made up of the remains of dead foraminifers!

Flagellates (FLA-jell-ets)

Flagellates, being protazoans, are, of course, also made of just one cell. But instead of forming pseudopods to get around, they have a whip-like tail called a **flagellum** (fluh-JELL-um). They wave their flagella (plural of flagellum) back and forth to push themselves through the water.

Many flagellates are green. They are green because they have chlorophyll in them, just like plants. And just like plants, the flagellates use their chlorophyll to make food and to release oxygen into the water. Besides using their chlorophyll, flagellates also have tiny "mouths." They use their flagella to scoop food into their "mouths."

Ciliates (SILL-ee-ets)

Instead of flagella, **ciliates** have tiny hairs called **cilia** (SILL-ee-uh) all around their outside walls. They move these cilia either to move themselves or to cause movements in the water around them so the water brings them the food they need.

The ciliates are usually bigger than either the sarcodines or the flagellates. Some can be more than a millimeter long. If you ever look in a drop of pond water, you are likely to find a **paramecium** or two. Some people have a special name for paramecia. They call them the slipper animalcules because they look a little like slippers!

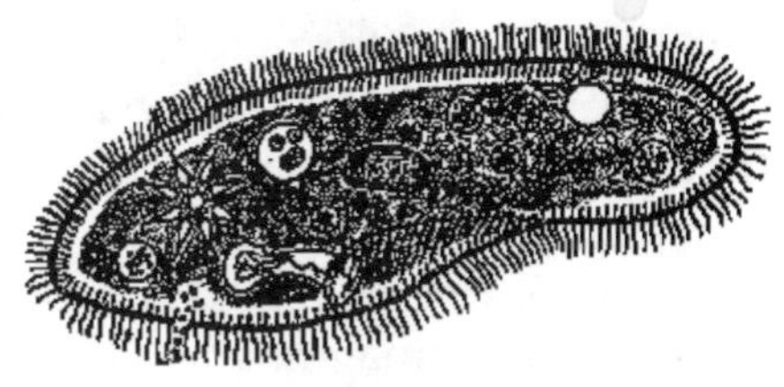

Unlike the amoeba, the paramecium dashes about its world with the help of the cilia that surround it. On one side (the bottom of the above picture), the paramecium has a primitive mouth. The cilia around the mouth help move food into the mouth.

Stentors

Stentors look a bit like trumpets or long cones. They usually use their narrow ends to hold onto an underwater plant, a piece of wood, or some other solid object. They use the cilia at the open end of the "trumpet" to wave water and food into their mouths. (Their mouths are at the open end of the trumpet.)

Vorticellas

Vorticellas (vor-tih-CHELL-uhs) are a bit like stentors. They, too, attach themselves to some solid object and they feed in much the same way: their cilia draw food into their mouths. Instead of looking like cones, however, vorticellas look more like tall wine glasses or flowers with extremely long stems. When things are going fine, the vorticellas have their stems extended all the way out.

It is common for many vorticellas to live close together. If the water they are living in happens to be disturbed, however, they will immediately pull their stems in, draw their heads back, and stop moving their cilia. They will then sit there, unmoving, for several moments. If you've been watching them, you can imagine them thinking to themselves: "Is someone out there trying to hurt me?" They don't move. But then, if nothing happens, one of them will stick its head up and move its cilia. And, it seems, the moment one does that, all the others get in on the act as well. Pretty soon the whole colony of vorticellas are back to work again, moving their cilia, trying to grab whatever food will come their way.

Vocabulary

protozoan—any of the one-celled creatures that are members of the protista kingdom

pseudopod—false foot; bulges in sarcodines' bodies that they use to help themselves move around, to eat, and to reproduce

cytoplasm—the jelly-like stuff that fills a cell

sarcodine—a protozoan that uses pseudopods

amoeba—a type of sarcodine

foraminifer—a protozoan that has pseudopods and that surrounds itself with a shell

flagellum—a whip-like tail that certain protozoans use to move themselves about

flagellate—the kind of protozoan that has a flagellum

cilia—little hair-like structures that surround the cell walls of some protozoans that they use to move themselves and/or to move the water in which they live

ciliate—the kind of protozoan that has cilia; ciliates are usually larger than either sarcodines or flagellates

paramecium—a common ciliate

stentor—a protozoan that is shaped like a trumpet; it has cilia around its mouth (the large end of the "trumpet") that it uses to move food into its mouth

vorticella—a protozoan that looks like a long-handled wine glass or flower; it usually lives in a colony with other vorticellas

Questions

1. How does a pseudopod work? *(The protozoan pushes out the wall of its body and fills the area with cytoplasm.)*
2. What good are pseudopods? *(A protozoan may use pseudopods to move its body, to acquire food, or to reproduce.)*
3. How do amoebas reproduce? *(They form two pseudopods that stretch in opposite directions; meanwhile, they duplicate their genetic information and send one copy to one pseudopod and the other to the other pseudopod; they then split down the middle and now there are two small amoebas where one large amoeba used to be.)*
4. How do amoebas stay alive when their environment becomes unhealthy for them? *(They pull in all their pseudopods and permit their cell walls to become thick and hard, protecting them from the hostile environment; they can remain "asleep" like this for months and even years.)*
5. How do some amoebas help human beings? *(The E. coli amoeba lives in our guts and helps us digest our food!)*
6. How do some amoebas harm human beings? *(The E. histolytica causes horrible diarrhea, and can kill a person.)*
7. Why are foraminifers important? *(Because their shells form the bulk of the chalk, limestone, and seafloor ooze in the world.)*
8. In what ways are many flagellates like plants? *(They have chlorophyll inside themselves and use that chlorophyll to manufacture their own food.)*

9. What is another name for the paramecium and why does it have this name? *(Slipper animalcule – because it looks a bit like a slipper.)*

THE BIG AND THE SMALL

Now that we have studied a bit about almost all the plants and animals in the world, I thought you might like to see a chart that compares the largest animals one with another, and another chart that compares the smallest protozoans.

May God bless you as you discover more about the wonderful world He has created!

A Few Large Animals

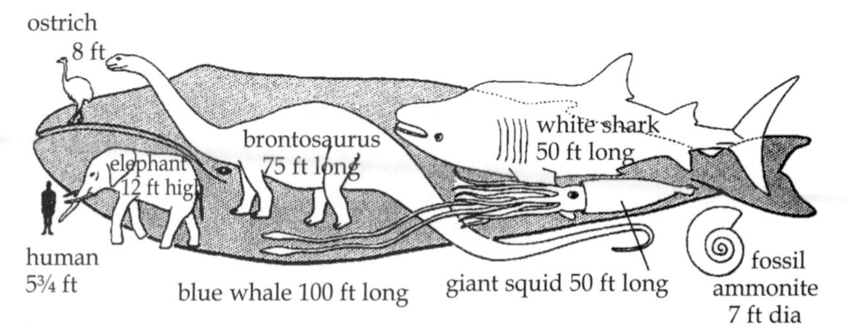

A Few of the Smallest Protozoans and Other Cells

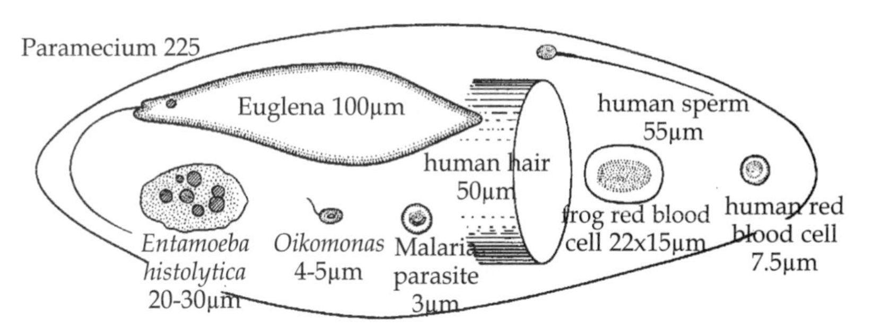

*μm stands for *micrometer*. One micrometer equals one one-thousandth of a millimeter or, put another way, one one-millionth of a meter.

BIBLIOGRAPHY

The following is an incomplete listing of the books consulted in producing *Introduction to Biology*. The books in bold type were of particular help. Most illustrations were adapted from Benson's and Drimmer's volumes.

Benson, Lyman. *Plant Classification* (Boston, MA: D. C. Heath & Company, 1957).

Bold, Harold C. *The Plant Kingdom*, 3rd edition (Englewood Cliffs, NJ: Prentice-Hall, Inc., 1970).

Drimmer, Frederick, ed. *The Animal Kingdom* (New York, NY: Greystone Press, 1954).

Hickman, Cleveland P. *Integrated Principles of Zoology* (St. Louis, MO: C. V. Mosby Company, 1979).

Lerner, Carol. *Plant Families* (New York, NY: William Morrow and Company, 1989).

Scagel, Robert F., et al. *An Evolutionary Survey of the Plant Kingdom* (Belmont, CA: Wadsworth Publishing Company, Inc., 1965).

Taylor, Ian T. *In the Minds of Men: Darwin and the New World Order* (Toronto, Canada: TFE Publishing, 1991).

World Book Encyclopedia, 1988 edition (Chicago, IL: World Book, Inc., 1987).

Adams, Clark E. "Flying squirrel."

Bennett, Albert F. "Snake."

Crowcroft, Peter. "Flying lemur."

Ernst, Carl H. "Lizard."

Ernst, Carl H. "Reptile."

Ernst, Carl H. "Turtle."

Ferguson, John C. "Echinoderm."

Harrison, Frederick W. "Sponge."

Huey, Raymond B. "Flying dragon."

Huey, Raymond B. "Tuatara."

Jones, Clyde. "Flying fox."

Ledbetter, Mary Lee S. "Protoplasm."

Mandell, Donald and Walker, Jerry T. "Plant."

Parkes, Kenneth C. "Bird."

Raven, Peter H., reviewer. "Flower."

Smith, C. Lavett. "Fish."

Van Gelder, Richard G. "Mammal."

Wit, Lawrence C. "Invertebrate."

Wit, Lawrence C. "Protozoan."